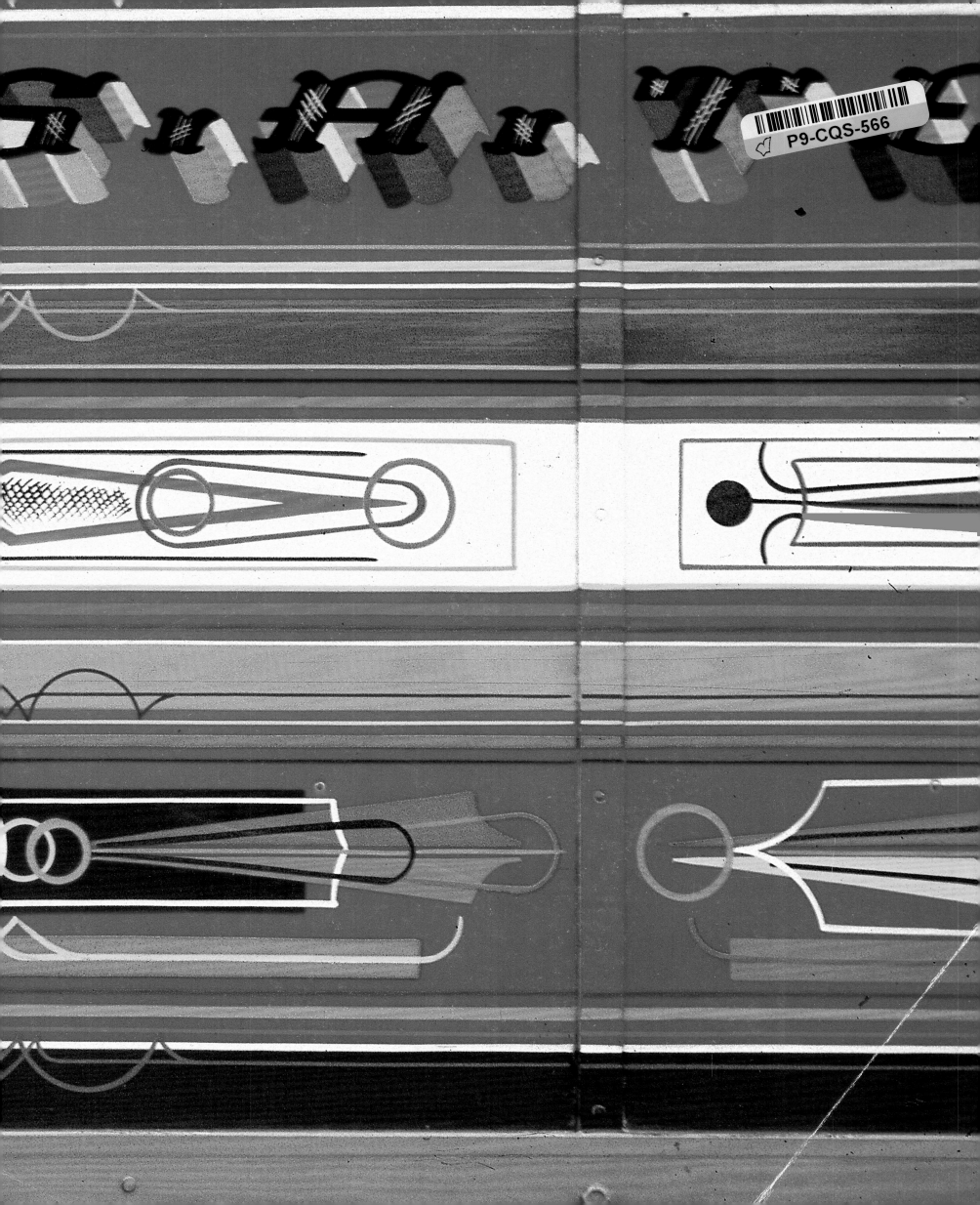

THIS IS
COLOMBIA

from Arcesio Perdomo
To Dr April
I hope you enjoy it!

ediciones
gamma

THIS IS
COLOMBIA

ediciones
gamma

AN EDICIONES GAMMA S.A. PUBLICATION

GENERAL MANAGER
   GUSTAVO CASADIEGO CADENA

EDITORIAL CONSULTANT
   ALEJANDRA GÁFARO REYES

MARKETING
   GERSA MEDIOS/GERTRUDIS DE SAPORTAS

EDITORIAL SUPERVISION AND DESIGN
   SANTIAGO MONTES VEIRA

ELECTRONIC ARTWORK
   JUAN PABLO MONCAYO GUERRERO, SANTIAGO BARRIGA AMAYA

RESEARCH
   ÁNGELA GARCÍA, RICARDO RODRÍGUEZ

TEXTS
   HELENA IRIARTE

ENGLISH VERSION
   PETER GOODHEW

PHOTOGRAPHY

   FABIÁN ALZATE
      4, 5, 6A, 14A, 14E, 19, 30A, 30B, 30C, 31A, 34A, 39A, 57A, 83A, 190C, 244, 249, 294C, 296, 301, 308B, 322, 333.

   LORENZO FONSECA
      GUARDA, 9C, 10, 13A, 13B, 13E, 16, 17, 21, 32B, 33A, 34D, 37A, 38E, 39F, 54, 55, 58A, 58B, 59A, 59D, 62A, 62B, 69, 71, 72, 77A, 77C, 77F, 79, 80, 93, 97B, 111B, 114B, 132, 133, 138A, 139A, 140B, 140C, 143, 148C, 151, 152, 154, 157, 158, 159, 162B, 162D, 163A, 163B, 163D, 168, 173D, 179A, 182, 184B, 184C, 184D, 185, 187, 190D, 192, 194A, 194B, 196A, 197A, 197B, 197D, 201A, 212B, 218B, 225C, 230, 231, 238B, 240D, 241A, 241B, 243, 251D, 254C, 254D, 258, 269B, 273B, 274A, 274B, 276, 277, 280, 281, 283, 284C, 284D, 288, 290, 291A, 291B, 291C, 328, 329, 340A.

   DORA FRANCO
      38C, 77B, 119B, 172B, 188, 196B, 197C, 199, 225B, 240B, 247, 248, 253A, 254B.

   ALVARO GUTIÉRREZ
      2, 3, 6B, 6C, 6D, 8, 9A, 9B, 9D, 13C, 13D, 14D, 26, 27, 38A, 38D, 39B, 48, 52, 53, 59C, 63, 76, 77E, 85A, 90, 128A, 153, 160, 161A, 161B, 166A, 166B, 170, 171, 173A, 183, 195A, 195B, 198, 203, 204, 205, 208, 209, 210A, 210C, 210D, 212A, 216, 218A, 220A, 220B, 221, 225A, 225D, 234B, 239B, 245, 251B, 252B, 254A, 273A, 284B, 286, 321, 326B, 338, 344, 345.

   ANDRÉS HURTADO
      18, 28, 29A, 29B, 31B, 31C, 200, 228, 232A, 232B, 233A, 238A, 240C, 241C, 241D.

   GERMÁN MONTES
      7, 22, 23, 24, 25, 32A, 33B, 34B, 34C, 36, 37B, 37C, 37D, 38B, 38F, 39D, 39E, 40, 41, 42, 45, 49, 50, 51, 57D, 57E, 58D, 59B, 60C, 60D, 68, 77D, 81, 83B, 88, 91, 92, 96, 97A, 102A, 102B, 102C, 102D, 128B, 129, 130, 131, 134, 135A, 135B, 138B, 139A, 140D, 141, 142, 145, 147A, 147B, 148D, 150A, 155, 156, 162A, 162C, 163C, 167, 169, 172, 173C, 178, 181A, 181B, 184A, 186, 189, 190A, 190B, 202, 210B, 226, 234A, 242, 246, 251A, 251C, 252A, 253B, 255, 256, 257, 259, 260, 261, 262, 263, 264, 265, 266A, 266B, 269A, 272, 275, 279, 282, 285, 289, 291D, 292, 293, 294A, 294B, 294D, 295, 297, 298, 302, 304, 306, 307, 308A, 308C, 308D, 309A, 309B, 309C, 309D, 310A, 310B, 311, 317, 318, 327, 330, 331, 332, 335, 336, 339, 340B, 340C.

   SANTIAGO MONTES
      43, 44, 46, 47, 56, 57B, 57C, 57F, 82, 229, 233B, 235, 236, 237A, 284A, 300, 303, 305, 312, 313B, 319, 341.

   MIGUEL MORALES
      5, 14B, 14C, 20, 35, 39C, 58C, 70, 78, 89, 104, 111A, 114A, 119A, 140A, 144, 146, 148A, 148B, 150B, 176, 179B, 180A, 180B, 201B, 227, 239A, 240A, 250, 278, 299, 314, 315, 316, 323A, 323B, 324A, 324B, 325, 326A, 334, 337, 340D, 342A, 342B, 343.

   I/M EDITORES ARCHIVE
      60A, 60B, 61A, 61B, 62C, 62D, 64, 73, 84, 85B, 127, 165A, 165B, 174A, 174B, 191A, 191B, 214, 217, 267.

   PUBLICITARY PHOTOGRAPHY
      GERMÁN MONTES, DORA FRANCO, HELLEN KARPF, NORA ELENA MÚNERA, LEÓN TRUJILLO, VIVIAN SAAD, JORGE MEJÍA, ANDRÉS LEJONA, SAUL MEZA, CARLOS ARTURO OSORIO, UBALDO CASTRILLÓN, LOPE MEDINA, MAURICIO ÁNJEL.

PHOTOMECHANICS
   ZETTA COMUNICADORES LTDA.

PRINTING
   D'VINNI EDITORIAL LTDA.

©   EDICIONES GAMMA S.A.

ISBN 958-9308-41-4

CONTENTS

PROLOGUE

Colombia, forwardmost corner of South America, possesses vantage points on the past and the present reaected in the Caribbean, and on the 21st century as it can be imagined from the Pacific coast. As the ariginal trunk of the region which witnessed the campaigns and glories of the Liberator, Simón Bolívar, Colombia was diminished in area by the separations of Venezuela and Ecuador after the wars of independence. Colombia was a leader in the emancipation movements of these countries and would continue —as did Argentina in the south— to play a key role in South American affairs. This importance had its beginnings during the Conquest, when the rapidly-developing colonies led the Spanish Crown to divide its original Viceroyalty of Peru into two new seats of power: that of Nueva Granada, with Santa Fe de Bogotá as its capital, and that of Río de la Plata, with its center at Buenos Aires. From that time until the present, these have been the two poles of the hemisphere's political life.

Although leading parallel lives, Argentina and Colombia have grown in very different ways. While Buenos Aires, a minute backwater for over two centuries, suddenly attained a fabulous growth rate when world commerce opened up and the republican period began, Santa Fe de Bogotá in 1800 only numbered 20,000 souls and in 1900 still hadn't reached 100,000. European emigrants swooped down on Buenos Aires, at certain times more numerously than to New York or to the United States as a whole. From its earlier status as a large town inhabited by citizens of pure Spanish stock, Buenos Aires became the Italian capital of the New World. In Bogotá, however, even a century after the birth of the Republic, a child of a non-Spaniard was a foreign rarity. This was partly explainable by the fact that Colombia is a vertical country and has grown most rapidly in the highlands. There were more Germans in Barranquilla and Bucaramanga than in Bogotá at the turn of the century. Too, the population did not grow because of waves of Euro-

pean immigration but because of the birth rate of the original settlers, whose families multiplied unplanned and without resources. Bogotá still had not reached one million inhabitants when Buenos Aires was already the largest city in Spanish America.

Today the goals of emigration are not those of the last century. Colombia's population is larger than Argentina's, and for the first time in Bogotá there are synagogues, many Protestant churches, and mosques. Because of Colombia's "verticalness," with three chains of the Andes dominating its high-relief geography from north to south, aviation has changed lifestyles. Today a traveler reaches Bogotá from Barranquilla after a one-hour flight, a sharp contrast with the two weeks or more needed fifty years ago to travel up rivers by boat and along stone paths on muleback. In Colombia airmail senrice began in 1919 and, since then, airline passenger and air cargo services are proportionally greater than those of any other country. In this question of geography, one should compare the country of the Andean north with the horizontal Argentina of the pampas which the English covered with a network of railroads. Because one traveled at mule-speed in Colombia, with frequent stops, many villages developed which are today's cities. The Republic has become a counhy of cities. There are one thousand townships at every geographical altitude, from those at sea level to settlements at 3,000 meters above it. Unlike Argentina, a country with seasons where cold and hot weather can be predicted by the calendar, Colombia's climate and seasons can be selected by traveling to the coasts or the highlands, with a driver at the wheel and a road map in hand. In an hour or two, one can go from a hot city —Cartagena, Buenaventura, Santa Marta— to a cold one like Bogotá, Tunja, or Pasto. Spring or autumn can be had according to one's whim, and landscapes can offer plantains and coconut palms and a tree called Macondo or the highlands' frailejón with its furry silvered leaves or—at a higher climb to the bleaker moors— the timid bluish potato flower.

Colombia's verticality is so impressive that travelers from the times of Humboldt and the intellectual Mutis of the Botanical Expedition to today's tourist agents have continued to praise what amazes every visitor: the natural resources of Colombia are more attractive, thrilling, and spectacular than its politics. In both there are poetry and violence. Politically speaking, there is no other country in the records of Spanish American evolution so profoundly born for civilian lifestyles than Colombia, and it is truly a marvel that the birth of a country oriented toward representative democracy would occur in the very entrails of the Bolivanan army. Francisco de Paula Santander, founder of the nation, said it all almost 200 years ago in words that have been carved in the marble of many universities and halls of justice even outside of Colombia: "If armaments have given you independence, laws will give you liberty." In contrast with this institutional pronouncement, periods of blood and violence have occurred, such as the civil wars of the 1880s or the guerrilla conflicts of today, together with the illegal drug trade. But the Republic has never lost its civilian mode of living. In nature, the same occurs with flora and fauna. When Bogotá was founded, the Conquistadors advanced up a river teeming with alligators and climbed the slopes of the Andean mountains through a land of jaguars, covered with leaves and roots and venemous snakes and enormous spiders that crawled beneath their toes. The men often went mad, after sleeping under the shade of the tree called borrachero. All of this was described fifty years ago by José Eustasio Rivera in a novel about the Amazon jungle whose title is apt: The Maelstrom (La Vorágine). The story tells of tiny mysterious fish which can devour a man in minutes and leave the skeleton floating in the water. Army ants advance, destroying whole forests. Even the toads sweat poison, deadly when used to anoint arrowheads. All of these can be found in the same country with the world's rarest and most beautiful orchids, with coffee plantations frosted with flowers that, drifting to the ground, perfume the valleys. These plantations produce the thickly-beaded berries —red to dark purple— that are roasted and ground in the preparation of the black beverage consumed throughout the world.

Today violence and the circumstance of Colombia's being part of the drug route have spread an image which surprises Colombians them selves more than foreigners. I don't believe that these developments can become entrenched in a country which has lived differently for five centuries. The answer is in the uninterrupted progress clearly visible in its great cities, three of over one million inhabitants and twenty of over one hundred thousand. Fifty years ago barefoot inhabitants disappeared from the scene. Dikes were built to provide water for villages, and electricity was generated through one of South America's most ambitious projects. And industries multiplied. Half a century ago, Bogotá had only a beer distillery and a glass factory. Leather exports were in the form of hides. Chairs were imported from Vienna, suits from London, china from Germany, crystal from Bohemia, mirrors from Venice. Today everything is produced and manufactured in Colombia. Medellín exports cotton cloth to the United States. Publishing houses make books for Italy and India. Shoes and purses are made for Europe. Bogotá is Colombia's largest industnal city, but Medellín, Cali and Barranquilla are equally important and factories multiply even in small municipalities. Exportation of flowers is growing in undreamed-of quantities.

There are presentations throughout the world of Colombian painting, music, dance, and literature, arts which amaze those who find only news about cocaine and kidnappings in the newspapers... crimes whose origins are international.

Today Bogotá's population is the same as New York's seventy years ago. A Colombian, García Márquez, has received the Nobel Prize in Literature. During the summer season, Cartagena is a paradise for tourists. The finest theater of America, Europe, and Japan is represented at the Bogotá Theater Festival. The bullrings of Bogotá, Manizales, and Cali host the finest bullfighters of Spain, Mexico, and Colombia. Virtuosos from two continents take part in the Popayán Music Festival. Colombia, remote and unknown in the last century, is now on the world map.

German Arciniegas

PRESENTATION

Welcome to Colombia, this beautiful tropical country which provides a great variety of contrasts, as much in its stunning landscapes, as in the customs of its inhabitants and the immensely rich biodiversity of its flora and fauna.

The cordillera of the Andes, which on entering the country divides into three huge branches: the Caribbean coast with the imposing Sierra Nevada de Santa Marta; the Pacific coast, with unexplored jungles, and Orinoquia and the Amazon, virgen and wild lands, are the natural regions which provide innumerable resources which, with its friendly, warm, hospitable and hard-working people, constitute Colombia's most important heritage on entering the 21st century.

The book which Ediciones Gamma has the pleasure of offering you provides an overall view of the country. It begins with an overview of its rich geography and continues with a description of its interesting historical process from when these climes first became populated. It illustrates the fascinating pre-Columbian cultures which developed refined pottery and gold working techniques, and analyzes the colonial and republican periods with their impressive architectural heritage, until arriving at present-day Colombia, sometimes vibrant and sometimes traditional.

In each of the eight regions in which the book is divided you can observe in detail the landscape, natural resources, agricultural production, the people and the accelerated and sometimes contradictory development of its cities. Here you will see the difference which still exists between the countryside and the towns, also the great diversity of cultures, customs, traditions, work habits and food, and the forms which daily life takes in Colombia, whose plurality is perhaps unique in the world.

In order to obtain an up-to-date view of Colombia, we have employed photographic work of excellent quality, produced during the last three years, and exhaustive research concerning each of the regions of the country. In order to facilitate consultation, we have organized the information in the different sections of the book with a scheme which introduces the subject with a text followed by a photographic sequence and explanatory captions. In this manner a work to be both read and looked at has been achieved.

Lastly, we wish to thank all those individuals and institutions which contributed to this publication, especially those who with detailed information about its activities helped to enrich the material which we present, and which pretends as best as possible to show the reality of the country. This is Colombia.

THE EDITORS

LAND
OF CONTRAST

From the air, Colombia seems to rise up out of the water, crossed by powerful mountain chains which, separated by valleys and broad rivers, fan out towards the north. To the south-east, the territory spreads out over an immense plain which makes up the Orinoquia region and the dense Amazon jungle.

Situated between the Tropics (from latitude 12°30' north to 4°13' south), three-quarters of Colombia is located in the northern hemisphere.

The nation shares borders with Panamá, Venezuela, Brazil, Peru, and Ecuador. It covers an area of 457.360 sq. miles, including islands belonging to it, and is the fourth largest nation in South America after Brazil, Argentina and Peru. It is the only South American country to have coastlines on both oceans: 1.000 miles on the Caribbean and 800 on the Pacific. Colombia has several islands, including the archipelago of San Andrés and Old Providence in the Caribbean, and Gorgona, Gorgonilla and Malpelo in the Pacific. As a result of its insular possessions, Colombia

Pages 16-17, panorama of the Eastern Cordillera.

Page 17 (inset), Old Providence Island in the Caribbean.

Page 18, glaciar in the Los Nevados National Nature Park.

Page 19, sunset over the Pacific Ocean.

has maritime limits with nations as far away as Costa Rica, Nicaragua, Honduras, Jamaica, Dominican Republic and Haiti.

Colombia possesses a part of the Amazon, considered to be the planet's largest «lung», sharing its two million square miles of jungle with Venezuela, Brazil and Peru. The Orinoquia, which makes up the vast plains of eastern Colombia, stretches as far as the border with Venezuela.

Colombia's geographic location as a meeting point of the three Americas, its borders with the two largest oceans in the world, and its particular condition of being simultaneously a Caribbean, Andean, and Amazonian country with natural riches revealing a great potential for exploitation, make it a privileged nation.

RELIEF

The cordillera of the Andes crosses South America like a great backbone very near to the Pacific coast. It enters Colombian territory on the border with Ecuador, where it forms the Nudo de los Pastos. A little further north, in the Colombian Massif, it divides into two branches: the Western and Central Cordilleras. From the Central Cordillera a third cordillera separates -

the Eastern Cordillera - which crosses the country diagonally, marking the limit between two very different regions: one being the Andean area and the Llanos Orientales, and the other the Amazon.

The Western Cordillera is the lowest of the three and second in length, being 680 miles long. Its western slopes are wide, gently sloping, and very rainy, since they condense the humidity of the Pacific Ocean. The Eastern Cordillera, on the other hand, is narrow and rugged. There are several high points on this cordillera such as Azufral Volcano (13.350 ft. above sea-level), the farallones of Cali (15.300 ft.), and the hills of Torrá (13.140 ft.), Tatamá (14.140 ft.) and Tamaná (15.740 ft.) in the northern part of the State of Risaralda. In the region of Antioquia, the cordillera reaches a height of 14.600 ft. above sea-level on the páramo of Frontino.

The Central Cordillera is the backbone of the Colombian Andes. It is the highest and oldest of the mountain system and has an average height of 11.460 ft. above sea-level. Over 600 miles long, it covers 42.460 sq. miles. The western slopes descend towards the valley of the Cauca River and the eastern slopes fall away

On page 20, the snow-capped volcano of Tolima forms part of
the Los Nevados National Nature Park, stands at 17.000 ft.,
and is situated very near the coffee region.

On this page, landscape of the Eastern Cordillera on descending from the highland
plain of Cundinamarca and Boyacá towards the Magdalena River Valley.

to the Magdalena River Valley. Its peaks include Galeras Volcano (15.300 ft. above sea-level) and Doña Juana Volcano (15.200 ft.), near the city of Pasto. The volcanoes of Sotará (16.400 ft.) and Puracé (16.630 ft.) lie in the Colombian Massif and to the north stand the volcanic snow peaks of Ruiz (20.050 ft.), Santa Isabel (18.260 ft.), Quindío (18.330 ft.) and Tolima (18.970 ft.), which make up Los Nevados National Natural Park.

The Eastern Cordillera is the youngest in the Colombian Andes and has a different origin from the other two: its relief is the result of the folding of the Guyanese Shield, which took place about 24 million years ago. The cordillera is 750 miles long with a maximum width of 155 miles. It has an average height of 9.750 ft. above sea-level and covers an area of 50.000 sq. miles. Here lie the highland plains of the Sabana de Bogotá (9.300 ft. above sea-level), Duitama-Sogamoso (9.020 ft.), Belén (9.500 ft.) and Santa Rosa (9.880 ft.), among others. Some of the principal high points are: the páramos of Guerrero (11.800 ft.) and Merchán (12.260 ft.),

Saboyá Crag (14,330 ft.), the páramo of Guántiva (15.490 ft.) and the Sierra Nevada del Cocuy, some of whose peaks are nearly 18.000 ft. high.

There are other mountain formations apart from the Andean system: the Sierra Nevada de Santa Marta, the highest coastal sierra in the world, with peaks over 20.000 ft. high which rise up from sea-level to their summit of perpetual snow over a distance of only 19 miles as the crow flies.

The María Hills and the Piojó Range rise up from the Caribbean plains. On the peninsula of La Guajira there are several hill ranges, at less than 3.500 ft.: Macuíra, Cosinas and Carpintero. The hill ranges of Baudó and Los Saltos are situated on the Pacific coast, separated from the Western Cordillera by the river basins of the Atrato and San Juan. According to some geologists, the Darien Hill Range is an extension of the Andean system which stretches towards Central America. In Colombia the range ends at Cabo Tiburón on the Caribbean coast, while its main branch continues on to Panama. To the south-east of

On this page: the Cauca River is the second longest river in the country and its river valley is one of the richest and most productive in Colombia.

On the following page: beaches of the Arauca River, which forms the border with Venezuela and is an important means of communication with the Colombian Llanos Orientales.

the country lies the Macarena Hill Range, incorporated as a National Nature Park. It is a formation independent of the Andean and Guyanese-Brazilian systems. It is 74 miles long and 19 miles at its widest point and its high points range from 1.800 to 5.400 ft. It is one of the oldest formations on Earth. The sierras of Chiribiquete and Araracuara in the Amazon are other important hill ranges. Covering nearly 5.000 sq. miles, the sierra of Chiribiquete is the largest preserved area in the country's National Nature Parks system. Some of its high points stand at over 3.500 ft. and its geological composition relate it to the hills of Araracuara and the Guyanese Shield.

HYDROGRAPHIC SYSTEM

Colombia is a country rich in water resources. Its numerous rivers represent a considerable potential for power generation, river transport, agriculture, fishing and recreation. Its hydrographic system is formed by four large basins: the Caribbean, Pacific, Catatumbo and Eastern, which some geographers subdivide into two: the Amazon Basin and that of the Orinoquia. The main rivers which which make up the inland hydrographic system rise in the Colombian Massif: the Magdalena, Cauca, Caquetá and Patía rivers.

The Caribbean basin, drained by the Magdalena and Cauca rivers, is the most important in Colombia. The Magdalena, the longest Andean river in South America, rises in the páramo de las Papas, at nearly 13.000 ft. and as it descends it receives the waters of its tributaries: the Páez, La Plata, Saldaña and Coello rivers which rise in the Central Cordillera, and further north the waters of the Gualí, Guarinó, La Miel, and Nare rivers. The Cabrera, Sumapaz and Bogotá rivers contribute their waters off the Eastern Cordillera. In this region the Magdalena River carries large quantities of sendiments and begins to form alluvial dams, channels and shallows, with the result that it continually changes its form. In the so-called Mompox Depression it receives the waters of its main tributary, the Cauca River, which together with the San Jorge and Cesar rivers forms an inland delta, whose labyrinth of waters makes up a systems of shallows, channels, *ciénagas* and

arms which disappear and reappear with the seasonal rising and falling of the water level. On leaving the Mompox Depression, the river continues until it flows out, after a journey of 960 miles, at Bocas de Ceniza, near the city of Barranquilla, supplying water to the Ciénaga Grande de Santa Marta through streams and lesser ciénagas. Previously known as the Río Grande de la Magdalena, the river is saturated in history, since it was for a long time the country's principal means of transport and the backbone of its development as a nation.

The Cauca River rises in the páramo de Sotará in the Andean Knot, and runs parallel to the Magdalena River in a valley between the Central and Western Cordilleras; 636 miles further on it flows into the Magdalena River. Along its course it receives the waters of the Piendamó, Ovejas, Palo and Man rivers, among others. Near to its source the river forms the rich valley which carries its name and then it flows through steep, narrow valleys between the cordilleras until it joins the Magdalena River.

Rivers which rise in the Sierra Nevada de Santa Marta also form part of the Caribbean basin. Some, such as the Don Diego, Dibulla and Ranchería rivers, flow directly into the Car-

ibbean; others, such as the Cesar River, flow into the Magdalena.

The Atrato River, which rises to the west of the Caribbean basin on Plateado Hill, at 10.500 ft., is one of the largest rivers in the world in relation to the size of its catchment area. After the Magdalena, Cauca and Atrato rivers, the most important river of the Caribbean basin is the Sinú River, which rises on Paramillo Heights in the Western Cordillera.

The main rivers which make up the Pacific basin rise in the Nudo de los Pastos, on the western slopes of the Western Cordillera and in the hill range of Baudó. The San Juan is the largest river and the Patía River the longest of the entire South American Pacific basin. The Atrato River rises near the San Juan River but flows into the Caribbean in the Gulf of Urabá. A hill range whose maximum height is 470 ft. forms the divide between the two catchment areas. Other important rivers in this basin are the Tapaje, Iscuandé, Guapi, Micay, Telembí, Yurumanquí, Raposo, Dagua, and Baudó rivers.

The Catatumbo basin, which forms part of the Caribbean catchment area, is formed by the Zulia, Táchira, Sardinata and Tarra rivers, tributaries of the Catatumbo River which flows into Lake Maracaibo in Venezuela, after flow-

ing through Colombian territory where it has its source.

The Eastern basin is formed by two main basins, those of the Orinoco and Amazon rivers, and covers 258.600 sq. miles of Colombian territory. The Orinoco catchment area is formed by the rivers which cross the Llanos Orientales and which are subject to rising and diminishing water levels according to rainfall. Those of the Amazon catchment area are jungle rivers, whose courses are fed by the high rainfall of the region, and are governed by a different climatic regime on account of their location in the southern hemisphere.

The Arauca River forms part of the border with Venezuela for 174 of its total 620 mile length. Together with the Meta, Vichada, Guaviare and Inírida rivers, it is one of the principal rivers of the Orinoco basin. The Vichada river rises in the Llanos Orientales and its course runs for 430 miles before flowing into the Orinoco River. The Guaviare River, 745 miles long, is formed by the waters of the Ariari and Guayabero rivers, which rise in the Eastern Cordillera to the south of the Macarena Hill Range. The Inírida River is a jungle river from its source.

An intricate river network makes up the Amazon River Basin: the Guainía River, flowing for 372 miles through Colombian territory, continues on into Venezuela where it is called the Black River. In the eastern border region, the Guainía forms the arm of the Casiquiare, a natural channel which connects the Orinoco and Amazon basins. Another important tributary of the Amazon is the Caquetá River which rises in the Colombian Massif, and during its 1.370 mile course receives the waters of the Orteguaza and Caguán rivers, among others. In the region bordering Brazil, the Caquetá River receives the waters of its principal Colombian tributary, the 750 mile-long Apaporis River. The Putumayo river rises in the Nudo de los Pastos, receives the waters of the Guamués River, its most important tributary, and flows into the Amazon in Brazilian territory. Its 1.120 mile course forms part of the border with Ecuador and the entire border between Colombia and Peru.

CLIMATE

Although Colombia is situated between the Tropics, the Andean mountain system gives it

*In the torrid zone, climate depends on altitude, which permits each region
to have a stable mean temperature throughout the year.
However there are wet or dry periods which slightly modify it.*

*On page 24: the Caribbean in Tayrona National Nature Park, and on this page,
different climatic zones in the Sierra Nevada de Santa Marta.*

a varied topography, which ranges from tropical rain forest and savannas at sea-level, to páramos and perpetual snow. Colombia's geo-astronomical position permits it to receive more or less constant solar radiation throughout the year, which is why day and night are of similar length, and why climatic variations are determined by altitude, trade winds, rainfall and humidity.

According to altitude, the mountain system divides into four bands, or climatic zones (temperature decreases about 2°F for every 1.000 ft.): hot (from 0 to 3.000 ft. above sea-level) with mean temperatures of around 77°F, covers 80% of the country; mild (from 3.000 to 6.500 ft. above sea-level) with mean temperatures between 65°F and 75°F, covers 10% of the country; cold (between 6.500 and 10.000 ft. above sea-level) with mean temperatures between 54°F and 64°F, constitutes 8% of the country; *páramo* (over 10.000 ft.) with mean temperatures below 54°F, represents 2% of the country.

There are extreme variations in rainfall in Colombia with regions such as Chocó in the north-west of the country receiving some of the highest rainfall and humidity levels on Earth (7.000 mm), and regions such

as La Guajira in the extreme north-east of the country, with a desert and steppe-like climate, spiny vegetation, high temperatures and scarce rainfall (400 mm. per year).

NATURAL REGIONS

Five natural geographical regions can be distinguished in Colombia for their particular physical and climatic characteristics, and the composition of their soils and vegetation:

a) The Caribbean region, the coastal area and vast inland savannas which are situated between the Caribbean and the northernmost spurs of the Andes. In gently rolling country (except for the Sierra Nevada de Santa Marta), high points barely reach 1.000 ft. above sea-level. The region is full of rivers, streams, ciénagas, and channels, shallows and flood plains, whose forms and sizes vary considerably. The climate is hot and the soil, semi-arid in parts, becomes desert in much of the peninsula of La Guajira.

The states of La Guajira, Cesar, Magdalena, Atlántico, Bolívar, Sucre, Córdoba and the northern part of the states of Antioquia and Chocó are situated in the Caribbean region, which include cities such as Cartagena, Santa Marta, Barranquilla, Riohacha, Valle-

dupar, Sincelejo, Montería and Mompox, islands such as San Andrés and Old Providence, the Rosary Islands and those of San Bernardo, and several other small islands and keys.

b) The Pacific region, with its wild coastal strip covered with jungle and mangrove swamps, is a humid region having one of the heaviest rainfalls on Earth. It stretches for 800 miles between the Colombia's borders with Panama and Ecuador. The seaboard is shared by the states of Chocó, Valle, Cauca and Nariño. This sparsely populated region has only one economically active city: Buenaventura, the most important seaport in the country. The second port on the coast is Tumaco, in the state of Nariño. The islands of Gorgona, Gorgonilla and Malpelo belong to this region.

c) The Andean region covers the three cordilleras, is the most densely populated and has attained a great degree of economic and social development.

The main cities of the region include Santafé de Bogotá, the nation's capital, Medellín, Cali, Popyán, Pasto, Manizales, Pereira, Armenia, Neiva, Ibagué, Tunja, Bucaramanga and Cúcuta.

d) The Llanos Orientales, or Orinoquia, include the states of Arauca, Casanare, Meta and Vichada. The Llanos of both Colombia and Venezuela make up the savannas of the Orinoco River. The region is sparsely populated and the majority of settlements are situated in the foothills of the Eastern Cordillera, as is the case of Villavicencio (the «gateway to the Llanos» and capital of the state of Meta), Acacías, Villanueva, Yopal and Tame. Oil fields discovered in Arauca and Casanare have attracted settlers to the Orinoquia.

e) The Colombian Amazon region.

It is larger than the Llanos Orientales and less populated. It covers the states of Caquetá, Putumayo, Guaviare, Vaupés, Guainía and Amazonas, over an area of 163.000 sq. miles. There are about 50.000 Indians dispersed in numerous communities which are situated near rivers crossing the Amazon jungle; settlers make up the rest of the population. The region has a high rainfall and humidity, and

Page 26: Colombia has is a sizeable portion of the Amazon, the dense and impenetrable jungle that is the Earth's lung and the area with the greatest number of vegetable and animal species.

Page 27: thanks to its geographical position, Colombia is the country with the largest number of bird species in the world - around 1.800.

the heat is constant throughout the year, which make it difficult for cattle ranching and agriculture. The most important city of the region is Leticia, capital of the state of Amazonas and a port on the Amazon River, at the border with Peru and Brazil.

FLORA AND FAUNA

Colombia's topographical characteristics make it a privileged nation with respect to biodiversity. Although representing less than 1% of the world's available land, Colombia shares with Peru third place in the greatest diversity of living species, after Madagascar and Brazil. Its location in the north-west corner of South America makes Colombia an obligatory point of interchange of fauna and of migratory cycles between North, Central and South America, and its varied geographical characteristics provide the necessary conditions for the emergence and development of a large quantity of vegetable and animal species. The country is considered

to be a sanctuary for one out of every five species of known fanerogams and possesses over half of the páramos in the world. To date 130.000 plants have been classified, of which about half are endemic. Colombia is famous for its flowers (with over 50.000 species) including the orchid - the national flower - of which there are some 3.000 varieties.

Colombia also possesses 15% of all land vertebrates. It occupies first place in the world in diversity of birds, with nearly 1.800 species of the 9.000 or so which exist on the planet. There are also 1.200 known species of marine life, 1.600 freshwater species, and an enormous variety of amphibians, reptiles, bats, rodents and insects, which are still being researched, notably butterflies with 165.000 species and coleopteros (beetles) with over 250.000 varieties. The typical fauna of the rain forest includes jaguars, armadillos, monkeys, snakes and a variety of bears, including the spectacled bear.

The Central Cordillera is eminently volcanic and has heights of over 17.000 ft. There are several snow-capped peaks here, such as those of Ruiz, Santa Isabel, Tolima and Huila. On the previous page, Laguna Verde in the Los Nevados National Nature Park, whose color is due to the sulphur emanating from the volcanoes.

On this page two aspects of the Ruiz snow peak can be seen: an icecap, and the Arenas crater which has a diameter of 2.500 ft. and emits fumes, indictating continuous volcanic activity.

Colombia is one of the few countries in the world possessing páramos, whose main function is to retain water which is accumulated in lakes and from where the major rivers of the country rise. On this page several aspects of the páramos of the Eastern Cordillera can be appreciated.

The hot climatic zone covers altitudes from sea level to 1.600 ft., ranging from desert regions
such as that of La Guajira to the heavy rainfall of the jungle regions of Chocó.

Page 36, Neguange Bay in Tayrona National Nature Park. On this page, above, San Andrés
Island in the Caribbean and Utría Sound on the Pacific Ocean. Below, Arauca River in the
Llanos Orientales and Cabo de la Vela on the peninsula of La Guajira.

Colombia is considered to be one of the world's richest countries in biodiversity. This is mainly due to its privileged position between the tropics, which gives it the entire range of climatic zones and an infinite variety of natural environments, where over 50.000 vegetable species are found, many of them endemic.

In the photographs the abundance of the tropics can be appreciated: a brightly-colored macaw, pineapples, a deer typical of the páramo region, an orchid (the national flower), a crocodile in its natural environment, and the platanillo flower.

The interchange of fauna between North, Central and South America contributes to the country having a large quantity of bird species (nearly 20%), more than 3.000 species of butterflies, and 8% of the animals found on the planet.
In the photographs:
flower of the freilejón, a typical plant of the páramo; flamingo, a migratory bird which abounds on the Caribbean coast; victoria regia, the largest water-lily in the world, found in the Amazon; a butterfly of the Monarch familiy; chontaduro fruit, and a hummingbird, a bird native to America, with 145 species found in Colombia.

FROM LEGEND
TO REALITY

The presence of American Man - as indicated by archeological evidence - is the result of Asiatic migrations which arrived on the American continent by different routes and in different eras. It seems that the first settlers arrived on the continent via the Bering Straits some 30.000 years ago according to conservative estimates, although there are those who consider it could have occurred about 100.000 years ago.

These migratory groups employed stone in a rudimentary fashion and based their economy on hunting and fruit collection. They spread out through America and the territory which today is Colombia, very probably following the course of the large rivers on whose banks lived the animals which made up their diet. The oldest remains of these Paleo-Indians in Colombia - who lived 13.500 years ago - have been found in the Andean region, at El Abra, near Zipaquirá (state of Cundinamarca), and close to the Tequendama Falls near the plains of Bogotá.

Around 3.500 BC, the migrations inhabited the coasts, lakes and rivers, broadening their diet with fish and seafood.

With the emergence of agricultural practices they began to become sedentary. The introduction of corn and beans in their diet, together with the product of hunting and fishing, left primitive man with time available, essential for the appearance of new activities such as weaving, gold and metal working, and advanced construction techniques. They developed a social and political organization, and perfected religious practice and a knowledge of astrology.

This process seems to have continued up until 1.000 AD, when as a result of the so-called «corn colonization», the high parts of the Andes began to be populated, which was later to give rise to more complex communities and to federations of villages such as those attained by the Muiska and Tayrona Indians.

GOLD-WORKING CULTURES

The pre-Columbian cultures of the present-day territory of Colombia achieved a high level of perfection in gold working, and the gold objects which have been preserved have aroused admiration throughout the world for the quality of the designs and the advanced tecniques employed in their manufacture. By studying different styles, specialists have identified two large

cultural regions, two general tendencies in which the techniques employed performed an outstanding role: the older one corresponds to the cultures of the south-west of Colombia and covers a broad zone which ranges from La Tolita on the northern coast of Ecuador, to the Quimbaya archeological zone. The pre-Columbian cultures of the Tumaco, Nariño, Tierradentro, San Agustín, Calima, Malagana, Tolima and Quimbaya tribes, manufactured gold objects with differentiated styles, but they generally employed a hammering technique, and embossing on fine gold lamina.

The second region, which covers the mountainous areas of the center-east and north of the country and the savannas of the Caribbean, was inhabited by groups belonging to advanced cultures: the Zenú, Muisca and Tayrona Indians. They preferred gold working techniques based on casting, which employed the lost wax process, a greater use of tumbage (a gold and copper alloy), and gilding by oxidation.

TAYRONA

The Tayrona Indians of the Sierra Nevada de Santa Marta began to become consolidated from the first centuries of our era, and attained their maximum splendor around the year 1.000 with

Page 44, the pre-Columbian Tayrona culture inhabited la Sierra Nevada de Santa Marta and was one of those which achieved the greatest perfection in gold work.

Page 45, it is thought that the «Infiernillo» near Villa de Leyva was an astronomical observatory of the Muiskas, one of the most advanced Indian groups in what is today Colombia.

the grouping together of numerous urban settlements, where they built terraces, retaining walls, drainage channels, paths, stairways and foundations for dwellings. Over 200 settlements have been discovered. They were accomplished weavers and potters, and their gold work is distinctive for being manufactured in tumbage cast with adornments of complicated design. Speaking the same chibcha tongue as the Muiska culture, the Tayronas maintained trading relations with communities in the lowlands, from which they obtained the gold which they lacked in the sierra.

SINÚ

The habitat of the oldest Indian culture known to date was the broad area of the Caribbean coastal plains, where the Zenú Indians established the first settlements in Colombian territory, occupying the valleys of the Sinú, San Jorge, Cauca and Nechí rivers. They drained the flood plains with a system of artificial canals which covered 2.000 sq. miles of marshland and which functioned for 2.000 years. This astonishing water management complex no only allowed them to control seasonal flooding, but also supplied them with abundant wild game and the irrigation

and fertilization of cultivated areas for a growing population. Its territory was divided into three large provinces governed by caciques who were related by kinship. The gold work of this culture is rich in lost wax techniques, hammering and false filigree work; the anthropomorphic and zoomorphic motifs and geometric designs were used for rituals, household goods, and as personal adornments.

MUISKA

Speaking the same chibcha tongue as the Tayronas, the Muiska Indians spread out across the eastern Andean highland plain from the year 600 up until the present era, organized in cacicazgos, which owed allegiance to two main chiefs: the Zipa of Bacatá and the Zaque of Tunja. The use of tumbage was due to the lack of gold. The gold objects of the Muiskas, preferibly used as votive offerings, are abundant; these objects called tunjos have been found on the highland plain around Bogotá and on the route which descends to the Magdalena River.

The sanctuaries where the offerings were deposited were situated in beautiful but remote spots. Lakes were the most important sanctuaries and served as the setting for solemn ceremonies

On this page, a burial chamber of the San Agustín culture,
whose monoliths were hewn in volcanic stone.

such as those which took place on Lake Guatavita when the new cacique received his investiture. This was the probable site where the legend of El Dorado originated.

TUMACO

The former inhabitants of Tumaco created a stable and varied social organization. Their dwellings were built on stilts on the islands formed by the inlets of the Pacific coast. Testimony to their way of life has been found in pottery figures which depict ornamented individuals, women, children, old people, dwellings and animals. The human figures display an accentuated deformation of the cranium, a symbol of distinction, which they practised in childhood by tying two pottery or wooden plaques to the front and back of the head. They mined gold and hammered and embossed it to produce masks, pectoral adornments, and figures with elongated craniums. They knew how to weld and took advantage of the properties of copper and silver.

CALIMA

The rivers which flow down from the Western Cordillera served as the point of access to the Andes. The Calima community settled on the banks of the Dagua and Calima rivers which fol- low the slopes of the cordillera as it descends to the middle valley of the Cauca River. These sedentary corn growers inhabited the area known as Calima in the Cauca Valley. From the first centuries of our era up until the year 1.000 they built terraces for dwellings, drainage channels, and paths which permitted them to trade with the Pacific coast. Their tombs, of different sizes, and the diversity of funeral objects, indicate a marked social stratification. They employed embossing and hammering techniques in their gold work to manufacture numerous large adornments. They also knew how to cast metal.

SAN AGUSTÍN

This is the most important archeological area in the country; it is situated in the Colombian Massif in a region of about 200 sq. miles. A few centuries before the present era, the former inhabitants populated a broad area where they built terraces for housing and crops, and artificial channels and mounds. Under these mounds stand monumental statues and tombs covered by heavy slabs, sarcophagi with rich belongings in gold and astonishing stone sculptures. It was a complex society, whose strength is expressed in the features of statues

which represent monstruous human beings, jaguars, birds of prey and snakes. Its privileged geographic location permitted this culture to use numerous waterways which linked them to such distant regions as the Amazon, the Pacific coast and the Cauca and Magdalena valleys.

TIERRADENTRO

Near the Colombian Massif, a rich natural region and the cradle of Colombia's rivers, emerged the culture of Tierradentro, which left its mark in the archeological remains located in the present-day districts of Inzá and Belalcázar, and especially around San Andrés de Pisimbalá, where the Archeological Park was built. This area is known for its tombs with underground chambers called hypogeums, some of them decorated with anthropomorphic and zoomorphic paintings and figures; here they placed urns containing the mortal remains.

NARIÑO

Between 800 and 1.000 AD, the highland plain in the far south-west of the country was inhabited by the Capulí culture, who buried their dead accompanied by splendid gold objects in tombs with a lateral chamber, up to 70 ft. deep. This culture maintained close commercial ties with settlers of the Amazon basin and the Pacific coast, from whom they obtained the coca leaves essential for daily life. Between the seventh and eighth centuries the plateau of Nariño was inhabited by the Piartal culture, notable for its advanced metallurgy, pottery and textiles. The Pastos and Quillacingas were rebellious tribes who were forced to pay tribute to the Incas. They dominated the area when the Spanish arrived and inhabited principally the slopes of the Puracé Volcano. They built their dwellings on mountain ridges and manufactured pottery, wooden and textile products, and fashioned gold objects of singular perfection.

TOLIMA

This region, located in the tropical lands of the middle valley of the Magdalena River, was an important passing point and an excellent site for trading goods. The Tolima culture expoited the rich alluvial gold deposits of the Saldaña River and surrounding areas. Its considerable mineral riches permitted an enormous production of gold objects and a broad trade with neighboring cultures, especially with the Muiska and

Quimbaya Indians. In addition to its gold production, the Tolima community left abundant pottery objects, among which funeral urns and vessels are notable.

QUIMBAYA

Situated on the moderate slopes of the Cauca River Valley, this region was inhabited, around the first millennium of our era, by a culture which produced gold work which was outstanding for its technical quality and designs. The Quimbaya Indians employed gold and copper alloy to cast both solid and hollow pieces, which have earned worldwide recognition for their perfection and beauty.

At the close of the past century a treasure was discovered in the region of Quindío which for the great quantity of objects was chosen as «honorary emissary» of the Colombian delegation at the exhibition which took place in Spain to mark the Fourth Centenary of the Discovery of America. The 'Quimbaya Treasure' was subsequently presented by the Colombian government to the Spanish Crown in recognition of its mediation in the boundary dispute between Colombia and Venezuela. Since then it is housed in the Museum of the Americas in Madrid.

THE INDIANS OF MALAGANA

At the close of 1992 a casual find opened an unusual chapter in the history of Colombian archeology. In the Cauca River Valley, where today sugar-cane plantations predominate, 2.000 years ago a hitherto unknown Indian community was settled, called the Señorío de Malagana. The art and technology of its gold and pottery objects reveal their elaborate symbolic thought and the dimension of their hierarchical society. According to dates produced by archeological analysis, between 240 BC and 70 AD the people of Malagana lived an era of splendor amidst a vigorous barter network with the neighboring Quimbaya, Calima, Tolima, San Agustín, Tierradentro, Nariño and Tumaco cultures.

The material remains of these pre-Columbian cultures, such as human bones, votive and funeral offerings, and artefacts for hunting, fishing and gathering, can be viewed at the National Museum and at the Casa del Marqués de San Jorge in Santafé de Bogotá. In addition, the magnificent gold legacy of these cultures can be admired in the Bogotá Gold Museum, where an impressive collection of over 33.000 pieces is kept. Archeological museums in other parts of the country also exhibit autochthonous values, and the Central Bank has distributed its collection to various of its branches in order to make it better known. In addition the Bank mounts exhibitions abroad to show the world Colombia's rich pre-Hispanic heritage.

DISCOVERY AND CONQUEST

Shortly after the discovery of America by Christopher Columbus in 1492, explorations on terra firma began, including the reconnaissance of the Caribbean coast of present-day Colombia.

While Columbus was still living, other expeditionaries obtained licences from the Spanish Crown, the so-called *capitulaciones*, to explore American islands and lands. So after traversing the Caribbean coast from La Guajira, the Spaniard Alonso de Ojeda founded San Sebastián de Urabá in 1509 in the north-west of the country, the first place to be settled by Europeans in these lands. In 1510 Vasco Núñez de Balboa founded Santa María la Antigua del Darién, from which he undertook an expedition which would lead him to discover the Pacific Ocean on the 1st of September 1513, which he called the «Other Sea».

In 1525, Rodrigo de Bastidas founded Santa

Marta, today the oldest town in the country, and discovered the mouth of the Magdalena River. Sailing up the «Rio Grande» signalled the commencement of the Conquest inland, encouraged by a vision of El Dorado, the mythical place where the Spanish supposed that gold abounded and which turned out to be the land of salt.

Several of today's principal cities in Colombia were founded during these years: Cartagena de Indias in 1533 by Pedro de Heredia; Cali and Popayán in 1536 and Pasto in 1539 by Sebastián de Belalcázar; and Santafé de Bogotá en 1538, by Gonzalo Jiménez de Quesada. With these settlements as a base, there began a systematic exploration of Nueva Granada, as this territory was called for its similarity to Granada of Spain, the region where Jiménez de Quesada came from. The expedition progressively established a complex network of settlements across the land, creating serious traumas in the native population which sometimes surrendered peacefully to the conquerors, on other occasions fiercely confronting them. Indian communities wanting to preserve their independence from the in-

Page 50, the maximum expression of military engineering in South America is the castle of San Felipe de Barajas, erected as a defense of the town of Cartagena.

Page 51, panorama of Villa de Leyva, one of the villages which preserves the architecture and urban layout of the Spanish town.

vaders ended up emigrating to the furthest corners of the country, where they have managed to preserve their culture up to the present day.

The Conquest was characterized by the plunder of Indian riches, the imposition of Spanish customs and beliefs, and by the exploitation of the Indian workforce, together with circumstances which gave rise to the «black legend», and which rapidly decimated entire Indian populations. This phenomemon gave rise to the introduction of a negro workforce from Africa, brought to the New World as slaves. The negro workforce was employed in the mines for their greater resistance and productivity, with the result that the African race became the third pillar of South American culture, through the cultural and racial mestizaje which today makes up Colombia.

THE COLONY

The anarchy and improvisation of the first decades of the Spanish occupation were due mostly to the difficulty which the Consejo de Indias experienced in ruling these lands from faraway Spain. This gave rise to a new legislation and a new conception of administrating the New

World, which laid the foundation of what is known as the Spanish Colony.

Once the lands were conquered and the Spanish had settled in towns and villages, what had been won had to be consolidated. Consequently, in 1557 the Real Audiencia del Nuevo Reino de Granada was set up in Santafé. The development of the American colonies, with the arrival of notables and lettered individuals, propitiated the creation of the first educational establishments, where descendants of the Spanish, called «criollos», were taught the arts, sciences and prevailing European philosophical thought. Slowly a road network was developed which permitted communication with distant provinces, and an important economy grew up centered on the mining of salt, coal, gold and emeralds, and later on quinine, indigo, and tobacco.

In 1739. Together with Peru and Nueva España (Mexico), the Viceroyalty supplied the Spanish Crown with enormous riches. The port of departure for the treasures of Nueva Granada was Cartagena de Indias on the Caribbean coast. This circumstance made the settlement a

coveted target for pirates and corsairs and explains its particular architecture as a fortified city.

Santa Marta, also on the Caribbean coast, preserves its colonial legacy from when it was the home of the first Governance of Terra Firme, spearhead of the conquest of the rest of the country, and where in 1830 the Liberator Simón Bolívar died.

In many of the villages founded during the Colony, examples of Spanish colonial architecture are still preserved, generally characterized by thick white walls on the outside of the houses, with imposing plastered wooden doorways and protruding balconies of painted wood. Numerous churches, chapels and temples are also preserved from this period, the majority built in baroque style.

The past is also preserved in the habitat of many other places in the country, such as Santafé de Bogotá, capital of the Nuevo Reino; Cartagena; Honda, a port on the Magdalena River which was an obligatory crossing point on the arduous climb to the capital; Tunja, the capital of the state of Boyacá, whose churches and colonial buildings are notable; Tópaga, and Monguí, and Villa de Leyva, which is noteworthy since it was chosen by Don Andrés Díaz Venero de Leyva in 1564 as the capital of the first Presidency, thanks to its geographical position and benevolent climate.

In the state of Santander there are numerous picturesque villages sprinkled across the state with such names as Barichara, Girón, San Gil, Charalá and Socorro, the birthplace of struggles for independence from Spain, and the region of the comuneros who in 1781 rose up against bad government and taxes, initiating the revolutionary process which was to culminate in 1819 with Colombia's proclamation of Independence. Further to the north-east, on the border with Venezuela, stands Cúcuta and Villa del Rosario, birthplace of Francisco de Paula Santander, the «Man of Laws» of the new republic and the home of the Congress which promulgated the Constitution of Colombia in 1821. Towards the south-west of the country the towns of Cali, center of the «confererated towns of Valle», and Popayán on the road to Quito and Lima - a vital component of the administrative, economic and cultural life of the Colony - preserve an important architectural heritage of the colonial period.

One of the most important cultural acts which took place during the Colony in Colombia was the Botanical Expedition - an inventory of the natural riches and advantages of the country for foreign trade - entrusted to the Spanish doctor and priest Don José Celestino Mutis. Between 1783 and 1816 Mutis and a group of co-workers explored the broad topography of the country to describe its geography, astronomy, mineralogy, medicine, zoology and botany, among other branches of science, and design means for developing the country.

But the work of the Botanical Expedition was interrupted first by the death of Mutis (1808), and then by the wars of independence (1810-1819). The collections and instruments were packed in trunks and sent to Madrid in 1816, during the «Pacification» which Pablo Morillo carried out in Colombia after the declaration of Independence in 1810. During this period many of the scientific mission's members, such as Francisco José de Caldas, Jorge Tadeo Lozano and Salvador Rizo were executed, or exiled, as in the case of Francisco Antonio Zea and Pedro Fermín de Vargas.

The cultural environment of Nueva Granada at the end of the eighteenth century was full of activity and enthusiasm. Several literary circles enlivened Santafé, where both local and foreign literature and scientific works were received, and journalism divulged news from abroad and from the different regions of Nueva Granada, creating a «reading trend» which disseminated the lights of the European Enlightenment and news of American Independence. The printing press was also active at this time. The most important publication, «The Rights of Man and Citizen», drawn up by the French Constitutional Assembly in 1789, was translated and reproduced by Antonio Nariño in his Imprenta Patriótica, but it earned him his exile. During the expedition which Baron von Humboldt undertook in Nueva Granada in 1801, he was able to confirm the independence sentiment of the population, its inconformity towards the policies of the Spanish Crown and the notable advance of naturalist studies.

INDEPENDENCE

At the dawn of the nineteenth century, independence winds began to blow throughout the American continent. On July 20, 1810, the cry of independence rang out in Santafé, as a result of which a provisional junta was set up. Shortly after the revolt had caught fire in different parts of the country, the Venezuelan Simón Bolívar arrived

Page 52, statue of Simón Bolívar in the Quinta de San Pedro Alejandrino, where the Liberator died on his way to voluntary exile, after failing to consolidate the Gran Colombia.

Page 53, gardens of Nariño Palace, seat of presidential power, situated in the historical center of Santafé de Bogotá.

in Colombian territory after having initiated armed struggle in his country and been defeated, joined the *criollo* armies of Nueva Granada.

The defeat of Napoleon at Leipzig in 1813 reinstated the despotic monarchy of Ferdinand VII of Spain, who in a desperate attempt to recover the lost domains abroad, sent a powerful military expedition under the command of Pablo Morillo to reconquer the territories in revolt. The expedition reached Venezuela in 1815 and initiated a reign of terror which earned Morillo the nickname of «Pacifier». With Juan Sámano installed as the new viceroy, the terror spread across the country as many of the rebels, the majority under the command of the young intellectual elite of Nueva Granada, faced the firing squad.

In spite of the initial successes of the Spanish army in its campaign of reconquest, in 1819 several battles were waged which ended in the defeat of the invading army. Notable are the battles of Pantano de Vargas, near Paipa in the state of Boyacá, and the battle of Puente de Boyacá, which was decisive in achieving liberty on August 7. A few days later the liberating army, headed by Bolívar and Santander, made its triumphal entry into the town of Santafé.

THE REPUBLIC

As a founding act in the Venezuelan village of Angostura on December 17, 1819, the political constitution creating the Republic of Colombia was issued, in recognition of the work of the Genovese sailor who died without having guessed at the real significance of his discovery for Europe, which was later to create a veritable New World. The Republic of Colombia was composed of Nueva Granada, the Capitanía General de Venezuela and the Presidencia de Quito, with its capital in Santafé de Bogotá and Simón Bolívar as its President.

In 1826 Bolívar, after handing over the government to General Santander following the Southern Campaign, returned to Santafé, but so large a country could not remain unified amidst the acute political antagonisms which were pulling it apart. In 1828 Bolívar was attacked in Santafé, and in 1830 he was deposed. His death, which occurred that same year, precipitated the dissolution of Gran Colombia. As a result, the independent nations of Venezuela, Ecuador and Colombia (Nueva Granada) emerged. Panamá remained part of Colombia until 1903.

The different ways of conceiving how the nation should be organized, the relationship between the State on the one hand, and the people, the Church and the provinces on the other, and the different interests involved, gave rise to multiple civil wars throughout the nineteenth century, during which six constitutions were issued and the country was given different names: República de Colombia (Gran Colombia) between 1819 and 1832; Nueva Granada between 1832 and 1858; Confederación Granadina between 1858 and 1863; and Estados Unidos de Colombia from 1863 to 1886. Finally in 1886 a centralist constitution gave birth to the present-day Republic of Colombia and which lasted for over a century, until 1991, when a Constitutional Assembly promulgated the new Constitution which today governs the Colombian people.

Around 1870, three-quarters of the country - the so-called «national territories» - were practically uninhabited, and immense fertile areas went unused, while the Eastern Cordillera sheltered 42% of the population. The colonization of this region was pressured by demographic and social problems common to the Andean region at the time. Three large areas of colonization during the second half of the nine-teenth century can be distinguished: a) Cattle ranching on the Caribbean hinterland. b) The coffee colonizations, which occurred in the region of Caldas and in the Cauca River Valley, undertaken from Antioquia, Cauca and Tolima. c) The exploitation of national forests: ivory palm in Chocó and Urabá, quinine in Cauca, Tolima, Caquetá and Santander, *palos de tinte* on the Caribbean coast, and rubber in Caquetá, Vichada, and Putumanyo, and to a lesser extent in Tolima.

The need to market the products of these new areas encouraged the construction of a network of roads and railways which would connect the different parts of the region with the river ports for the transport of the products to the sea, and then onwards to world markets.

The railway was synonymous with progress and all the provinces and regions of the country eagerly tried to lay their own networks for the transport of goods and passengers.

The Magdalena River was the nation's main artery and means of communication, until 1865, when the first telegraph line was inaugurated. A decade later, three lines ran from Bogotá to Antioquia, Cauca and the Caribbean coast. Thus the nation became progressively integrated, breaking the isolation which the topography had imposed on the country for so long.

Colombia entered the coffee market when consumption became popular in Europe and the USA - since 1918 the USA had become the world's leading consumer country. In spite of the recovery of gold and silver production after 1885, coffee was the product which put Colombia on the map of international trade at the close of the nineteenth century. National production and its marketing enabled the creation of capital which the country needed in order to industrialize.

A separatist movement, supported by a United States government interested in building an inter-oceanic canal in Panama under its control, led to the segregation of the province of Panama in 1903. As indemnity, Colombia received 25 million dollars, which began to arrive in 1922 and was principally used to build the physical infrastructure. The public works undertaken encouraged migration to the cities, and since then the population distribution began to shift in favor of the urban centers, which day by day grew in population. Around 1920 Santafé de Bogotá became consolidadted as the financial capital

of Colombia, and the headquarters of important national and foreign banks.

The second half of the twentieth century saw the National Front experiment flourish (1958-1974), which was an agreement between the two political parties, Liberal and Conservative, to alternate in power, in an attempt to end authoritarianism and political violence. The Constitution of 1991 was proposed by the National Constitutional Assembly to respond to a latent need: broaden participative democracy, achieve peace, end impunity, and create a way for the State to be led by honest and competent leaders. The recognition of human rights, the protection of ethnic minorities, the filling of important government offices through general elections, and administrative autonomy for districts and regions, are some of the most relevant subjects of the new Constitution. It provided the society and the State with agencies of control such as a Public Prosecutor's Office, an Attorney General's Office, a Constitutional Court, a People's Defense Authority, and other legal figures such as the *tutela*, which for the Colombian people is one of the most important instruments with which to achieve their common dreams.

At many spots in Colombia you can appreciate marvelous vestiges of pre-Columbian cultures: page 56, Ciudad Perdida in the Sierra Nevada de Santa Marta. Page 57, monoliths at San Agustin; gold votive offering of the Muiska culture; stairway to a hipogeum at Tierradentro; pectoral adornment of the Calima culture; burial urns; anthropozoomorphic pectoral adornment, Tayrona culture.

The Spanish Colony left many magnificent examples of civil, religious and military architecture in the towns of Colombia. Belfry of the church in the plaza mayor of Villa de Leyva. Balcony of a house in Cartagena de Indias. Cloister of the convent of Santo Ecce Homo near Villa de Leyva. Plazoleta Rufino José Cuervo, in the barrio of La Candelaria in Santafé de Bogotá.

Fortified wall in Cartagena de Indias. Central square of the convent of San Francisco in Santiago de Cali. Likeness of the Devil on the doorway of a colonial house in Cartagena de Indias. Narrow street in Honda, a port on the Magdalena River.

In the main cities of the country there are beautiful examples of Republican Architecture.

Top: *Panoramic view of Popayán downtown.*

Bottom: *Detail of the Cundinamarca State Government Building in Santafé de Bogotá.*

Republican Architecture is present in most of the houses in the Manga neighborhood in Cartagena.

Top: The magnificent mansion of the Román family.

Bottom: The School of the Sisters of Assumption in Manizales, the most important city in the Coffee Belt.

*The development of a modern Colombia continues taking advantage of the inexhaustible
resources which the country is endowed by nature. On this page: train which transports coal
in La Guajira; José María Córdova airport in Medellín; the port of Barranquilla and the
Cartagena de Indias Convention Center.*

Page 63, panorama of the center of Medellín.

HISTORY OF TELECOM

1. On May 23, 1947, the Empresa Nacional de Telecomunicaciones - TELECOM was set up by Decree 1684, for the purpose of unifying the telephone, radiophone and telegraphic services.

2. On Abril 13, 1950, the national government promulgated Decree No.1233 which merged the state institutions Empresa Nacional de Radiotelecomunicaciones, created in 1943 and the Empresa Nacional de Telecomunicaciones (1947).

3. Colombia commenced a TELEX service through TELECOM (1954), which consisted of the direct transmission of written messages between a sender and a receiver possessing equipment which permits the sender to directly type his message and the receiver to receive it typed on his machine, even without the presence of the operator.

4. In 1964, by Resolution 3861 the Ministry of Education approved the ITEC as an establishment for teaching, researching and disseminating relative sciences and communications and authorized it to offer the diploma of Higher Technician in Electronics and Communications.

5. On August 7, 1968, President Carlos Lleras Restrepo inaugurated the nation's Microwave Trunking Network.

6. In 1970 TELECOM inaugurated the Chocontá Earth Station which enabled satellite communication with the rest of the world.

7. In Bogotá, on Febuary 27, 1973, the president of TELECOM Francisco Lozano Valcálcer inaugurated the «Florentino Vezga» Building, the institution's new headquarters in the carrera 13 with calle 23. From 1975 on, the Plazoleta Adyacente has been adorned with a sculpture by Alejandro Obregón, titled «Releasing the Wavelength».

8. In 1990 the Trans-Caribbean Fiber Optic Submarine Cable was inaugurated, which offers greater quality, volume, velocity and fidelity in communications.

9. In 1995 an important technological investment was consolidated: the Management Networks, construction was begun of the Digital Fiber Optic Trunking Network, and CAPITEL was created in association with FEC, NORTEL, ERICSSON AND SIEMENS.

TELECOM TODAY

TELECOM as a long-distance national and international operator becomes transformed into a dynamic company capable of providing a wide range of products in accordance with the needs and expectations which customers have from day to day, in everything concerning solutions in telecommunications in Colombia.

FIBER OPTICS: Down our immense National Fiber Optic Trunk Route, 3.700 miles long and nine large metropolitan rings, television signals, information, voice, internet, and and multimedia will run at the fantastic velocity of light, that is to say at 340.000 kilometers per second, and the miracle of total interactivity will occur. Thus the dream of Colombia' Super Information Highway will come true.

TEVEANDINA: It is the most extensive regional channel in Colombia. 14 states connected to Bogotá and the most dynamic market in the country, exerting influence on the borders between four countries, and supported by the latest technology.

CAPITEL LOCAL TELEPHONE SERVICE: Along the 2.5 million local telephone lines that we will install in the large cities, will run, in addition to voice, the new services of added value, television on demand, internet, purchasing in virtual supermarkets, information, etc..., which will radically modify the way of life of the Colombian people.

INTERNET: Reduce its elitist character and its costs and place the worldwide network within everybody's reach are the main goals which will allow us to attain our great wish: to make the miracle of all Colombians interacting with the great Internet web a reality.

Our TELECOM Internet web will cross boundaries and spread across Colombia. The new generations will greatly change their way of thinking and their attitudes. They will become more tolerant, participate more and become more democratic.

For this reason our network, in addition to providing access and a carrier service, will make strategic alliances to provide content for formal education in schools, universities and for professionals of small and medium companies.

Our strategic alliances are being developed together with the Ministry of Education, the Secretariats of Education, and the large national and regional newpapers, with the aim of achieving our goal. Social internet will encourage the creation of «internet cafés» throughout the country, with special rates for telecommunications employees and students. It will also allow 2.000 state schools to acquire low-cost Internet and a telephone line as part of social telephony.

TELECOM IN THE FUTURE

THE INTEGRATED MANAGEMENT OF TELECOMMUNICATIONS, becomes a differentiating factor in a competitive environment, characterized by the accelerated technological evolution, de-regulation, liberation, the globalization of markets, diversification of services and the demanding requirements which customers place on these services. In this context, TELECOM began the construction and operation of a Master Management Plan, geared towards satisfying the needs and surpassing the expectations of its customers, through the re-designing of its operative processes and the provision of adequate tools to increase quality, efficiency and promptness in the delivery of services, and replace them in case of failure; all this at less cost and in the least time possible.

A hierarchical pyramid of integrated management systems was structured which covers: Business Management, Service Management, Network Management, and Network Elements Management.

LOW ORBITING SATELLITES, a constellation of 56 low orbiting satellites, which will circle the Earth at an altitude of 530 miles, will enable communications to be made without networks and with maximum security against interception.

This system guarantees the footprint of a satellite as a minimum, so that no communication has limits. No place on the planet will impide it, not the densest jungle nor the broadest desert. Thus it will be possible to make national and international calls from any part of the world with a «personal telephone», that is to say, with a unique universal number.

In addition, low orbiting satellites will be the best solution for one of the goals we have been proposing for 50 years: rural telephony.

The goal is to install public or community telephones in places where a minimum of 50 people live.

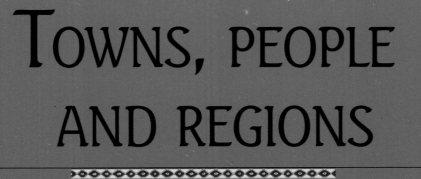

Towns, people and Regions

For its notable diversity of climatic zones resulting from its three cordilleras, its immense natural riches, its broad coastal regions on the Atlantic and Pacific Oceans, its jungles and savannas, mountains and valleys, Colombia possesses a multitude of natural environments which give life and particular traits to the people who inhabit each of these regions.

Of Colombia's nearly 36 million inhabitants, over 70% live in towns and cities and the rest in rural areas. The most densely populated area is the Andean region which houses 75% of the population. The Caribbean coastal region follows with 21%, while the Pacific region, together with the regions of Orinoquia and the Amazon, are home to a scarce 4% of the population.

Colombia is a nation of towns, and although Santafé de Bogotá is the seat of power and public administration, and generates a large part of the nation's riches, there are other cities which make important contributions: Medellín, one of nation's the most modern and beautiful cities, is impor-

tant for its industry and commerce; Cali, the hub of the sugar-refining industry, is an important cultural center and is home to a broad range of national and international sports events. The city of Barranquilla, pioneer of commercial aviation and home to one of the most outstanding literary and artistic groups of this century, has over the years preserved intact its folklore and popular traditions, brilliantly represented by its famous carnival. . Other regional capitals and towns have developed their own sources of riches, tourist attractions and commercial activities which generate considerable development at both regional and national levels.

Another aspect of Colombia, a nation of contrasts, are the particular traits of the inhabitants of each region, in their customs, traditions, myths and beliefs; in the local cuisine; in their folklore - song, dance and musical instruments; and in their particular way of speaking or keeping silence, a reflection of their approach to life, of communicating with others, with the surrounding nature and with God.

The immense majority of Colombia's population is the fruit of a marked process of *mestizaje*, the result of a blood mix between Spanish colonizers, Indians, and Negroes brought as slaves from the African coasts during the sixteenth and seventeenth centuries. However, in certain areas of the country Indian tribes continue to exist, which as a result of inhabiting isolated areas they have not been acculturated. Others, although having lost some of their customs and having acquired certain habits from outside, continue to preserve the essence of their beliefs, traditions and ways of contemplating the universe.

This mix of races and cultures contributes to Colombia's marvellous diversity and rich folklore which make up a wonderful mosaic and is one of the country's most appreciated attractions. Each of the regions, the highland region of the states of Cundinamarca and Boyacá, the Santander states, the Caribbean coast, the state of Antioquia and the coffee region, the Pacific cast, the south-west of the country, the Upper Magdalena region, the Orinoquia and the Amazon, have developed their own cultures and ways of life.

GIMNASIO BRITÁNICO

The British School is a bilingual (Spanish/English) college preparatory day school for some 3600 pre-school through high school students located in the scenic savanna region of Chía, Colombia. Ranked number one in Cundinamarca by the Instituto Colombiano para la Educación Superior, the school occupies nearly 136,000 square meters and encompasses nineteen buildings with extensive indoor and outdoor athletic facilities and ready access to a 155-horse riding stable. A new aquatic center with an indoor Olympic-sized swimming pool and diving pool will open on the campus in the fall of the year 2000. An International Relations Department, headquartered in Indianapolis, Indiana, U.S.A., oversees exchange programs

This new 1999 structure houses classrooms, laboratories and a Conference Center.

Uniformed students begin their day in the High School Building.

for seniors and recent graduates and summer camp programs for students aged nine to sixteen years.

Founded by Dr. Jorge Piraquive and Dr. Angela García de Piraquive in 1982, The British School today employs 300 support staff and upwards of 400 faculty, most of whom hold Master's degrees in their areas of specialization. In keeping with the school's stated mission to provide the best possible bilingual education for its students in scientific, humanistic, and cultural areas, all facilities are continually updated and technological support expanded to enable students to compete nationally and internationally in every area of endeavor. A new test center housing 60 computers opened in July of 1998 and construction of a new academic building was completed in January of 1999.

75

Sports and physical fitness are viewed as essential components of the educational process at The British School, and abundant opportunity is provided for exercise, training and competition. There are six soccer fields and one regulation competition field with viewing stands surrounded by a competition-quality running track, several prepared surface tracks surrounding the practice fields, seven outdoor basketball courts, three tennis courts, and three large gymnasia divided between two buildings. In addition, the large campus allows for numerous play areas with up-to-date playground equipment and wide open spaces for the enjoyment and physical education of young students. Equestrian training is available for children aged eight years and

Elementary students enjoy one of several playgrounds and recreational sports areas.

up, while aquatic sports and events coaching is available for all students aged five years and older.

Academically rigorous programs for pre-school through high school are coordinated to provide an integrated curriculum and the foundations for a lifelong learning pattern that has become the hallmark of the school. The goal of faculty and administrators is not only to promote intellectual growth and high standards of personal excellence, but also to instill in their students essential values such as compassion, respect, integrity, and commitment. Virtually all graduates of The British School go on to college or professional school for which they have been well-prepared to compete in an increasingly complex and diverse world

Elevated stone walkway connecting academic buildings.

On this page: market day in Buenaventura harbor.

Page. 77, Wayúu Indians on the peninsula of La Guajira; elderly couple in the coffee region;
Guambiano Indians on a typical bus in the state of Cauca; vallenato singer with his
accordion; carnival participant in Barranquilla; country
person from the state of Cundinamarca.

HIGHLAND PLAIN OF CUNDINAMARCA-BOYACÁ, AND SANTANDER STATES

The highland plain of the states of Cundinamarca and Boyacá, located at the center of the Colombia, has a benign clmate and is surrounded by mountains which protect it from winds. It is a fertile land, rich in water resources, and was the territory of the Muiska Indian culture, one of the most advanced that the Spanish found on arriving in the territory that is now Colombia.

The three Conquerers whose expeditions penetrated the South American continent along different routes, drawn by the legend which spoke of fabulous riches at a place known only as El Dorado, were Sebastián de Belalcázar, who coming

Panorama of Tinjacá, Boyacá.

Page 80, the diet of the inhabitants of Boyacá, formerly populated by the Muiska Indians, was based on corn, today an extensive crop and source of income for farmers in the state.

Page 81, Indian and Spanish heritage is present in the colors of the houses of Ráquira, the «village of pots».

up from the south had already founded settlements such as Cali and Popayán; Nicolás de Federmán who was en route from the plains of Venezuela; and Gonzalo Jiménez de Quesada. In 1538 they coincided at the place which had already been chosen by Jiménez de Quesada for the founding of Santa Fe de Bogotá, the settlement which was to become the center of government of an immense terrritory called the Nuevo Reino de Granada.

The Indian population which inhabited this region was not very warlike, for which reason it was easily reduced to servitude. The population was well organized into political and administrative areas and had a social hierarchy which enabled the Spanish to exploit their labor and oblige them to pay tribute.

The Muisca Indians bartered to obtain gold from other tribes in lowland areas in exchange for salt, emeralds and fine cotton blankets. They fashioned sacred offerings, replicas of household goods which were buried with the deceased,

and diverse objects which were worn as ornaments.

Spanish towns were established on the sites of the Indian settlements of the Zaque and the Zipa, and progressed rapidly since they were the home of rich encomenderos who during the Colony and at the beginning of the Republican period endowed the settlements with the necessary infrastructure for them to become lettered towns, where leaders in the ecclesiastic and civil administration of Nuevo Reino de Granada were formed.

The majority of the state of Cundinamarca is mountainous and its relief corresponds to the Eastern Cordillera, its maximum height (15,000 ft. above sea-level) corresponding to the páramo of Sumapaz in the south-west. There are also hot lowlands in the Magdalena River Valley and in the foothills of the Llanos Orientales.

The State of Cundinamarca was founded in 1811, Jorge Tadeo Lozano becoming its first president. After Colombia's independence from Spain in 1819, the

departamento of Cundi-namarca was created which covered the entire country, acquiring its present-day limits from 1886 on. Industry, commerce, services and cattle ranching are some of the most important activities of the state, and the distribution of the resources is concentrated in Bogotá, whose industrial capacity is the greatest in the country both in terms of its importance and for the number of industrial firms established there. The agricultural sector and the flower-growing and cattle-ranching sectors are the most developed in the country.

The highland plain of Bogotá is connected to the state of Boyacá by a series of small valleys devoted mainly to «cold-climate» agriculture and dairying around small villages. The climatic and geographical conditions of the state of Boyacá make it the nation's leading grower of potatoes and onions. The region is also rich in the production of corn, wheat, barley, plantain and yucca.

The industrial development of Boyacá is centered on steel milling, cement and beverages. Mining has also played an important role in the economic development of the state with the extraction iron, phosphates, limestone, coal and emeralds. These were important before the Spanish Conquest, not only for bartering with the lowland tribes -for their cotton and gold, but in addition - together with gold and copper - formed part of their tribute to the gods, and for the manufacture of funeral objects.

To the north-east of the valleys of Ubaté, Chiquinquirá and Sogamoso, the Eastern Cordillera overlooks the valleys of the Suárez, Fonce and Chicamocha rivers which run off the hill range of the Lloriquíes.

The states of Santander and Norte de Santander lie to the north of Boyacá. During colonial times the region was an obligatory stopping place on the road which led to the Caribbean and to Venezuela, and from the seventeenth century on and until well into the nineteenth century the prosperity of the towns of Santander continued to increase. San Gil, Socorro, Girón, Bucaramanga, Pamplona, Ocaña, Villa del Rosario and Cúcuta grew both in importance and in material and cultural riches, and they competed with each other to provide the best living conditions for their inhabitants.

Page 82, the region of Santander is sprinkled with villages whose charm and elegance is preserved in their houses, their plazas and their churches, true relics of colonial art; panorama of Barichara.

Page 83, (above) Sierra Nevada del Cocuy and (below), canyon of the Chicamocha River, two of the most important geographical features of the region and the nation.

In the state of Santander, the Eastern Cordillera forms the Nudo de Santurbán where it forks: the western branch continues on through Colombia while the eastern branch enters Venezuela in the state of Táchira, and to the north the hill range of the Motilones marks the border between Colombia and Venezuela, in the state of Zulia.

In 1781 an uprising took place in the town of Socorro, which together with that of Tupac Amaru in Peru, was one of the first independence initiatives in Spain's South American colonies. It was sparked off by excessive taxation, since the region was a leading producer of tobacco and fabrics. The movement was put down and its leader, José Antonio Galán, executed. However, the seeds of liberty were to bear fruit with the commencement, a few years later in 1810, of the struggle for national liberation.

The rough and challenging topography soon obliged the settlers to confront extraordinary natural obstacles, which they have progressively managed to overcome, and the Santander states became one of the most prosperous regions of the country - this in spite of diffi-

culties which during the nineteenth century gave rise to civil wars (as a result of which Santander was created), the struggle against the Indians, and the contradictions which developed between German immigrants - advocates of free trade - and crafts guilds which were to opposed to it.

A rich racial and cultural mix, the result of Indian, Spanish and German contributions, makes up the Santander character: persistent in his work, moderate in his private life, an untiring fighter, and with a great sense of responsability towards his family and to his social obligations.

One of the most relevant aspects of industrialization in the region was the appearance of the oil enclave of Barrancabermeja, which developed as a oil producing and refining center at the beginning of the twentieth century. In 1922 the Tropical Oil Company began large-scale commercial production, as a result of which several hundred workers from all over the country arrived in the area. At the same time the Andean pipeline was built, which was to carry crude oil from Barrancabermeja to Cartagena.

One of the main characteristics of the highland plain of Cundinamarca-Boyacá is the presence of the "páramo" system, a strongly humid environment.

In the photograph, the Iguaque high barren plain in Boyacá.

In the plains of Bogotá and the state of Boyacá, there is a great abundance of small towns which still preserve the legacy of the Spanish Colony.

In the photographs, panoramic of the plain in the north of Bogotá and the Tópaga Park in Boyacá.

In harmony with nature, the Politécnico Grancolombiano is located on the eastern hills of
Santafé de Bogotá, surrounded by broad green zones. Its educational system by cycles
provides technological and professional degrees which are taught as day and night courses.
University postgraduate programs are offered as night courses. Its internet address is:
http://www.poligran.edu.co

FEMEC began as an Integral Cooperative of Associated Medical Work, and after almost five years of being founded by sixty visionary doctors it has made important achievements, such as reaching a population of around 4.000 members, doctors and dentists, its establishment as a source of work, and a leading position in worldwide cooperativism through the International Cooperative Alliance ACI, and the International Health Cooperatives Organization IHCO.

FEMEC also develops ambitious educational programs through its magazine Revista Femec de Medicina and its Noticias Femec bulletin and develops academic postgraduate programs with different universities. Its Health Promotion and Illness Prevention program, and the Medical Auditing program, are models which enjoy ready acceptance in the country and abroad.

And since its diverse activities are centered on Social Security in Health, it has led a thriving business complex consisting of the Health Promoter Institution UNIMEC S.A., USIFEM, a company which provides support technologies for the medical profession, and the USIMEC Cooperative, formed by the users, who through it can help themselves with respect to needs derived from illness.

Santafé de Bogotá

Good land! Good land!
Land that puts an end to our suffering.
Land of gold, blessed land
Land to make our lifelong home,...
Juan de Castellanos

The expedition which under the command of Gonzalo Jiménez de Quesada penetrated the territory of present-day Colombia, started out from Santa Marta with five hundred men. After enduring all kinds of suffering, they found clear evidence of civilization when two members of the expedition brought Jiménez de Quesada Indian cotton blankets and salt loaves, a sign that the end of their suffering was at hand.

Quesada arrived with 166 men in a land where corn, potato, yucca, and bean crops were plentiful, grouped around a large number of circular dwellings. The land of the Muiska Indians was named Nuevo Reino de Granada and on August 6, 1538, Santa Fe was founded. Friar Domingo de las Casas was said to have officiated the first mass. The *plaza mayor* was established between two of the rivers which flowed down off the mountains, the San Francisco and San Agustín rivers, and the church and government offices were erected on their banks.

Given the benevolent climate, fertile soil and abundant Indian labor which was soon distributed between the *encomiendas* granted to Jiménez de Quesada and the members of the expedition, Santa Fe grew in importance. In 1550 it became the seat of the Real Audiencia and the capital of the viceroyship of the Nueva Granada in 1739, which generated a concentration of political power. From July 20, 1810, onwards, it was the site of the worst repression inflicted by the Spaniards Pablo Morillo and Juan Sámano during the so-called «age of terror», until 1819, when the country finally gained independence from Spain.

During the nineteenth century the city was the scene of civil disturbances which followed emancipation. It was declared the capital of Gran Colombia, and although this was dissolved in 1830, the city continued to be the capital through successive political changes until in 1886 it was named the capital of the Republic of Colombia. At the dawn of the twentieth century, during a period of po-

litical peace, it began its transformation into a modern city. Bogotá lived through the painful events of April 9, 1948, when as a result of the assassination of the political leader Jorge Eliécer Gaitán, the center of the city was almost completely destroyed.

URBAN DEVELOPMENT

The small, isolated and rather provincial city modified its urban structure: banks, commerce and aristocratic family residences moved from the center to other areas which within a few years gave rise to commercial, residential and business sectors.

Its continuous growth soon made it necessary to build roads to facilitate traffic. The first was the Avenida Caracas, in the 1930s, followed by the Autopista del Norte, and the bridges of calle 26 and carrera 10. From then on the city has expanded to cover a large part of the surrounding plain, annexing villages such as Usaquén, Suba, Usme, Fontibón, Bosa and Engativá. Its present population numbers 7 million inhabitants.

DIVERSITY MAKES FOR HARMONY

To the east, Bogotá is lined by a chain of hills, among which Monserrate stands out, on the top of which stands a church and is a place of pilgrimage, and from where a magnificent view of the city can be had.

New buildings have appeared near the traditional barrios, which have made Santafé de Bogotá a city of contrasts. In the old barrios many large houses have been restored, today home to foundations, government offices, museums and auditoriums. Part of the colonial architecture has been preserved in houses of Andalusian style and in the city's extraordinary churches and beautiful republican buildings.

Examples include the former Jesuit complex made up of San Bartolomé, the church of San Ignacio, and the seminary of Las Aulas - today the Colonial Art Museum and the Palace of San Carlos; the Coin House, built in the seventeenth century, where the ovens for forging gold and silver coins were housed; the Religious Art Museum; the house of the Marqués de San Jorge where the Archeological Museum functions; the 20 de Julio Museum, known as the Casa del Florero, where the brawl which sparked off the uprising of 1810 took place; the Astronomical Observatory; and the Colón Theater, for whose construction eminent Italian architects, sculptors and decorators were hired. At different points in the city center there are also

Page 90, at the top of Monserrate, one of the main hills of Santafé de Bogotá, stands the church, a place of pilgrimage for the inhabitants of the city.

Page 91, the barrio of La Candelaria, its streets lined by Andalusian houses, preserves all the charm of the colonial period.

magnificent examples of republican architecture such as the Echeverry Palace and the government offices of the state of Cundinamarca.

SECTORIZATION OF THE CITY

Traditional barrios such as Egipto and La Candalaria make up the city center, together with the space around which the city was founded in 1538, and which has since then been the setting for Bogotá's most notable events. Until 1821 it was called the Plaza Mayor, then the Plaza de la Constitución, and finally with the erection of a bronze statue of the Liberator Simón Bolívar - the work of Italian sculptor Tenerani - it was named the Plaza de Bolívar. As in the colonial city, on the sides of the plaza stand the symbols of power: on the east side stands the Catedral Primada and the Archbishop's Palace; on the south side the Capitolium, seat of legislative power and where the presidents of the Republic take possession; on the north side, the Palace of Justice; and on the west side, the Liévano Building which is used as the city's Town Hall. Santander Park lies a little further north, gathering around it examples of architecture from different eras: the Central Bank building, the modern Gold Museum,

the Avianca building and three Franciscan churches.

The International Center has large modern buildings occupied by financial institutions, banks and hotels, the Gonzalo Jiménez de Quesada Convention Center and Bavaria Central Park. To one side of the towering buildings stands the old church of San Diego, colonial in style, the Bull Ring in Mudejar style, and the former prison, built in the nineteenth century, today home to the National Museum.

The most modern sectors are found mainly in the northern and north-eastern parts of the city, especially the buildings which line the Avenida Chile and which make up an important financial sector - among which buildings the old Franciscan church of La Porciúncula still stands. The calle 100 and carrera 7 to the north, among many other roads, are important thoroughfares lined by modern office blocks and large hospitals. Shopping malls have also contributed to the city: the first to appear was Unicentro, followed by Granahorrar, Hacienda Santa Bárbara, Bulevar, Andino and many others, which provide attractions for shoppers and offer a variety of entertainment spots.

All kinds of events, fairs and exhibitions attracting the different productive, technical, and agricultural sectors, including industry, crafts, publishing and many others, take place in the grounds of Corferias, which has excellent facilities consisting of modern and functional pavilions and conference rooms, perfectly equipped for both national and international events.

The city's industrial development can be witnessed in the Industrial Zone, situated in the south-west of the capital, with its immense manufacturing complex and warehouses. On the plain surrounding Bogotá an extensive and highly technified cultivation of flowers - considered to be the most beautiful in the world - has been developed, constituting one of Colombia's principal exports.

CULTURAL ACTIVITY

Since the eighteenth century, Bogotá has been a cultural center, giving birth to such important undertakings as the Botanical Expedition and the Comisión Corográfica, which traveled across most of the country making maps and illustrating the nation's customs and cultural expressions in excellent sketches, today housed at the National Museum.

Bogotá has magnificent cultural institutions, notably museums such as the Gold Museum, whose pre-Columbian gold collection is the most important in the world; the National Museum, which holds collections of archeology, ethnology and works of art of every period; the Religious Art Museum, the Museum of Popular Art and Traditions, the Modern Art Museum, the Quinta de Bolívar (the country home of the Liberator), the El Chicó Museum in the former hacienda of the same name, and many art galleries; libraries such as the National Library and the Luis Angel Arango Library; theaters such as the Colón, Jorge Elécer Gaitán, Colsubsidio, and Libre theaters, and auditoriums such as the music room of the Luis Angel Arango Library, one of the best in South America, and the León de Greiff and Camarín del Carmen auditoriums; the cultural center of the Gimnasio Moderno School, and the Skandia Cultural Center; at all of which, important orchestras, chamber groups, artists, and theater and opera companies of international standing perform.

URBAN LIVING

Santafé de Bogotá is today a modern city, where its inhabitants have access to a variety of cultural events, recreation and relaxation. It has several sports centers

such as the Campín, with a stadium and coliseum, and El Salitre, which has a fun park, a coliseum, free sports facilities and a water toboggan. In Simón Bolívar Park there is a lake for watersports, athletic tracks, bicycle paths and a large plaza where sports competitions and cultural events are held.

On Sundays and holidays, the inhabitants of the city can go roller skating, trotting, bicycling or simply walk down the main avenues which become bicycle routes protected by the metropolitan police for the security of children and all those who wish to rest from the noise and congestion. Thanks to programs provided by the Town Hall, cultural and recreational events take place in the different parks, thus strengthening a sense of community.

At nightfall the city lights up and a multitude of places open their doors, where you can enjoy an excellent meal or eat informally and dance to the sound of different rhythms. Nighttime activity is very lively in places such as the International Center, the Zona Rosa, the north of the city and nearby villages.

AROUND AND ABOUT THE CITY

Santafé de Bogotá is surrounded by villages which preserve their traditional charm and provide healthy relaxation for those who go out on Sundays to take a rest from the city and enjoy the beautiful and peaceful countryside. Along the northbound trunk road which crosses the highland plain there are recreational parks, lakes such as that of Fúquene and the legendary Guatavita, and reservoirs such as Tominé, Sisga, and Neusa, where you can go camping and enjoy sailing and other watersports. Near the city lie the villages of Chía, Cajicá, Tabio and Tenjo and the town of Zipaquirá, famous for the salt deposits which the Muiska Indians exploited and for the Salt Cathedral, a true jewel hewn in the rock salt, unique throughout the world.

Near to Bogotá you can also enjoy the exuberance of the tropics and discover another climate, changing vegetation and different kind of recreation. To the south or west and in only a few hours, you reach «cool-country» villages such as La Vega, Fusagasugá or Villeta, ideal for enjoying the sun and restfulness and the exotic fruits of the region, and Guaduas, a village which preserves its historical flavor, or continue on to the «hot country» of the Magdalena River Valley and spend the weekend at one of the excellent hotels at Melgar or Girardot.

The Fundación Universidad Central de Santafé de Bogotá, founded in 1966, is a non-profit, private university which fulfills a public service, with the purpose of creating professional quality and academic excellence, and with the greatest respect for individual rights and the social function of the State, with full and responsible university autonomy.

The University seeks to provide integral education with special emphasis on ethical and humanistic formation and on the knowledge and identification of Latin American reality.

The University has achieved national and international recognition for its academic and research quality, the social scope of its programs, the development of an institutional culture open to and respectful of the diverse ethnic and linguistic manifestations, and for the training of individuals committed to the development of the country in the different areas of knowledge, by means of the use and continuous renovation of advanced technologies.

COMCAJA (Caja de Compensación Familiar Campesina) is the only institution of its kind in Colombia with national coverage. It extends the benefits of the social security to the rural sector, offering quality services and programs that attend the basic needs of the affiliated members: education and training, health, recreation, tourism, housing, assistance for small businesses, and subsidy.

COMCAJA's flagship program, called "Promotion of Health and Prevention of Illness", concentrates on family health. The work teams, which include medical doctors, nurses, dentists, bacteriologists, professionals in the social area, and social workers, visit the rural and urban affiliated households. COMCAJA's health system has become the leader among the subsidy regimen institutions in Colombia. It offers to its 500.000 affiliates a national coverage health program focused on the family.

The Housing and Construction Department offers, to those affiliates whose monthly income does not exceed four minimum wages, a meaningful subsidy to improve used dwellings. Besides, social housing projects are being undertaken in the states of Casanare, Meta, Boyacá, and Cundinamarca.

COMCAJA is committed to an educational mission. Its goal is to guarantee the peaceful coexistence between citizens, and to prevent violence, in order to improve the quality of life. COMCAJA runs twenty-five education centers which cover the preschool, elementary and secondary levels. Besides, it has signed agreements with national institutions in order to give academic formation and technical training to its affiliates.

COMCAJA has many touristic and recreational facilities: COMCAJA Hotel in Girardot, Laguna Vieja Vacation Center in Yopal, and Los Bambués Vacation Center in Piedecuesta (state of Santander). It is currently adapting La Vallenata Park in Valledupar, and building a vacation complex in Coveñas.

Recently, COMCAJA received from the Government the license to open six drugstores, four of which are already operating in the cities of Barranquilla, Sincelejo, Tumaco, and Yopal. During the second half of 1998 two more will be opened in Pereira and Ciénaga. The development plan contemplates the opening of six additional drugstores, and by 1999 COMCAJA expects to run twenty-two drugstores in the locations that are most convenient for its affiliates.

Page 96, calle 11, one of the most traditional of the barrio of La Candelaria, with the cathedral tower in the background.

Page 97, the church-museum of Santa Clara was built between 1629 and 1674. Its interior decoration is the result of one of the main principles of American baroque art, abhorrence of a vacuum.

Interior courtyard of the House of Nariño, seat of presidential power.

Central Square, Colegio Mayor de Nuestra Señora del Rosario.

The Colegio Mayor de Nuestra Señora del Rosario, founded in 1653, has carried out without interruption its educational work at all levels, from primary and secondary school to the eleven university faculties which include undergraduate studies, specializations, masters and doctorates. Its motto is «nova et vetera» «Always Old and Always New» since its tradition, rooted in the universities of Bolonia and Salamanca, joins a great effort to achieve the mission of providing a solid ethical and humanistic formation which, linked to research and to the demands of knowledge, produces positive leaders who act to benefit Colombian society.

The coat of arms of the Colegio Mayor de Nuestra Señora del Rosario, engraved on stone.

The main lecture hall.

Graduation ceremony.

Colegio Mayor de Nuestra Señora del Rosario, interior view.

Interior of the cloister.

Facade of La Bordadita.

Weathervane on the facade of La Bordadita, the College's chapel.

Facade of the Colegio Mayor de Nuestra Señora del Rosario.

Page 102, Santafé de Bogotá has been since the Colony a city wih an intense cultural activity, including museums, theaters, churches and educational centers.

(Above) House of the Marqués de San Jorge, the home of the Archeological Museum. Wall of the Camarín del Carmen, today an auditorium for music and theater.

(Below) Archbishop's Palace and plazoleta of the San Bartolomé School. Facade of the National Museum, the most important and most comprehensive in the country.

Founded in 1580, the Santo Tomás University occupied for many centuries the place where the Murillo Toro Building stands today, in downtown Bogotá. It was closed in 1861 and reopened in 1964. Since then it has grown in Bogotá and has extended through all the country with great success. Today, in 34 regional centers, the distance education service offers seven degrees in Education conferred by the Faculty of Humanities, four technical and four professional degrees conferred by the Faculty of Sciences and Technology, eleven postgraduate certificate programs, and two master programs. In Bogotá it offers twelve undergraduate programs and twenty postgraduate programs, plus those offered by the distance education service. For all these reasons, Santo Tomás continues to be the first higher education institution in Colombia.

The International Center of Santafé de Bogotá has been witness to the modernization of the city; the Tequendama Hotel, one of the most traditional of the city, and the beautiful colonial church of San Diego, are seen amidst modern buildings, the headquarters of financial and commercial institutions.

Colombians need more and better financial services which enable them to satisfy their economic needs. This is the goal of the Banco Superior, a leader in personal banking, which offers a complete and practical portfolio with products designed for today's world. Among them Diners Club, the first credit card in Colombia.

INTERNATIONAL FAIR - BOGOTÁ -

Every two years Bogotá hosts the International Fair, organized by Corferias. In 1998 the Fair arrived to its XXII version. It is opened to many sectors of the economy, giving special importance to the capital and intermediate goods. At least thirty countries and more than two thousand exhibitors will be present in this important event.

The Corporación de Ferias y Exposiciones S.A. Corferias is a public company whose chief shareholder is the Bogotá Chamber of Commerce.

It has belonged to the International Union of Fairs (UFI) since 1954, the year it began to operate by putting on the Bogotá International Fair, which since its commencment became one of the most prestigious events in Latin America.

Over 25 events take place annually which bring together around 6.500 exhibitors and more than 1.000.000 visitors from all over the world.

For almost half a century, Corferias has become consolidated as an important sales showcase which possesses a modern commercial area with a total area of 150.400 m2 of which 68.325 m2 comprise a covered exhibition area, distributed in 27 pavilions and 166.020 m2 of open air exhibition space. Given the structure of its facilities, alternative fairs can take place simultaneously.

There are complementary services which include the modern register of buyers and visitors, an ample food plazoleta, a building for parking and a large convention center.

During almost 87 years, the Casa Editorial El Tiempo has been distinguished for the quality of its publications and the effectiveness of these as printed media. Today it is leader in Colombia in information, education and diversion. It employs over 2.600 people in several cities, which include Cali and Barranquilla where it has modern printing systems connected to the main Bogotá plant by a private satellite network. The El Tiempo Publishing House acts in three sectors: media, with El Tiempo - of greatest national circulation - and Portafolio - leader in the economy and business segment - , the Aló magazine, regional weekly newspapers and the new interactive and digital products of the electronic era; a distribution center which specializes in book sale channels (Circulo de Lectores), videos (Video Factory) and music (Tower Records); and in a third sector which manages data bases for business use. It also has interests in TV Cable, the multinational Beterlsmann with the Printer printing press, Trunking Movilink and the satellite television supplier SKY.

On Park Way amidst tall trees stands Chalet Suizo, a restaurant which has been appreciated for years by the inhabitants of Bogotá.

The effectiveness of the service, friendly attention, the great flavor of each of its dishes and a menu with the best Swiss and international cuisine, make Chalet Suizo the perfect spot to spend an excellent evening.

Its facade best identifies this restaurant, which brings through its dishes a little of Switzerland to Santafé de Bogotá. Chalet Suizo's ideal is for the inhabitants of Bogotá to spend time in the city and enjoy it, since there are suitable spots for every occasion, appropriate for relaxation. One of the main characteristics of this prestigious restaurant is its antiquity, since for over 45 years it has delighted the inhabitants of Bogotá with exquisite dishes, in addition to offering a friendly service to the visitor, who from the moment he arrives discovers a pleasant ambience. Chalet Suizo provides its services daily.

*The Santamaría bullring, a beautiful construction in Mudejar syle, where one of the most
important bullfighting seasons in the country is held, framed by the Torres del Parque.
Important figures in bull-fighting have performed in this bullring such as Manolete, El Viti,
Luis Miguel Dominguín, Pepe Cáceres and César Rincón.*

The Manuela Beltrán University was founded in 1975 as a technical high education institution. Nowadays, 23 years later, it offers professional programs in the areas of Health, Engineering and Education (approved by the resolution 18778 of the Ministry of Education, December 15, 1992).

The University offers undergraduate programs in Psychology, Physiotherapy, Occupational Therapy, Respiratory Therapy, Special Education, Computer Engineering, Industrial Engineering, Biological Resources Engineering, Environmental Health Engineering, Biomedical Engineering and Electronic Engineering. There are also twelve postgraduate certificate programs and six postgraduate diploma programs, all of which contribute to the formation of excellent professionals.

The virtual libraries, based in the Bogotá and Bucaramanga campuses, provide access to an enormous amount of electronic documents. Besides the

loan of these documents, the students can take advantage of many other services, such as videotext and videoconference. The University has become a leading institution in the use of the new technologies applied to education.

Some of the facilities of the University can be used both by the students and the public. Among these are UMBTV, a broadcast station approved by the Ministry of Education and Inravisión (the Radio and Television National Institute), and UMB Didáctica, whose main task is to develop and produce educational interactive material for the teaching of anatomy (medical illustrations, anatomical models and simulators). The University runs occupational health prevention programs in many companies and education centers.

The new campus of Santa Fe de Bogotá is located in the heart of the university zone of the city (avenida Circunvalar and calle 60). The intelligent buildings and the facilities in general were designed to satisfy the needs of the students and to give them comfort. Thus, Manuela Beltrán is becoming "the university of the future".

Since the 1960 AVESCO began activities with a store on Calle 63 with Caracas Avenue. Shortly after, new outlets began business, conserving the architecture of each sector, such as the outlet of San Diego.

AVESCO thus became one of the most vigorous in the country, becoming well-established in the food sector. At present it possesses over 100 outlets in the main cities. Up-to-date equipment for producing fast foods, such as continuous processing lines and individual rapid freezing which guarantee product quality, form part of the most modern food production plant in South America. During its 28 years of activity, AVESCO has created around 56.000 direct and indirect jobs, has trained its employees and families, has promoted a better quality of life by making contributions to housing, health and education, and has been successful in giving impetus to the market.

In Santafé de Bogotá there are great contrasts and different architectural styles. (Left) the colonial church of San Diego and in the background the Seguros Tequendama building, in the International Center. (Right), the Avenida Chile, in the north of the city, an important financial and business center where buildings of other eras coexist; in the foreground the church of the Porciúncula and behind it the Granahorrar shopping mall.

It is located 35 minutes from the El Dorado International Airport, two blocks from the Avenida Chile Financial and Business Center and near the large shopping malls.

It has 430 rooms -single, double, junior suites, suites, executive floor- equipped with a mini-bar, coffee pot, international television, hair dryer, security key and deposit box. There is 24 hours room service as well.

You can enjoy the best food in the restaurant "Harem" and a pleasant cocktail in the Lobby Piano Bar, in addition to room service.

The Convention Center has as part of its facilities an Auditorium, a Large Reception Room, Foyer, Meeting Rooms and Private Rooms, audiovisual aids, sound system, large projection screens and special staging.

The Holiday Inn Select Hotel & Convention Center, has Aiport-Hotel-Airport transport and provides Reception, Valet Parking, Travel Agency, Currency Exchange, Security and Gymnasium.

The Universidad Sergio Arboleda was founded in 1984 for the purpose of training professionals in science, the academic world and culture, with a creative and critical spirit and engaged in the economic, social and cultural development of the country.

As a result a leading institution has been achieved in the strengthening of professional work in Colombia and the integral formation in social, ethical, scientific, technical and humanistic areas, with a vision not only towards the national but also international setting.

The following programs are at present undertaken: Law, Philosophy and the Humanities, Languages and Classical Literature, Social Communication and Journalism, Business Administration, Finances and Foreign Trade, Economy and International Banking, Industrial Engineering and Mathematics.

One of the most important places is the bookshop, where recent national and foreign publications, reference works, newspapers, magazines, videos, and encyclopedias in CD ROM can be perused and acquired, and, most especially, books published by the University Publishing Fund.

CENTRO COMERCIAL HACIENDA SANTA BÁRBARA

On the Royal way to Tunja, exactly at the gates of the distant village of Usaquén, a magnificent house of Spanish style was built in 1847. It had a beautiful arc at the entrance, a chapel, wide gardens, fountains, dappled corridors and stables.

140 years later, in 1987, this old mansion, already restored and declared a National Monument, became the base for the construction of the most spectacular shopping mall: the Centro Comercial Hacienda Santa Bárbara which, thanks to a humanist architectural concept, harmonizes tradition and modernism in the way its 400 commercial sites show.

At the Hacienda Santa Bárbara ecology is a reality all around its broad space for gardens, fountains, squares and centennial trees.

All these aspects make the Hacienda Santa Bárbara the top shopping mall in Santa Fe de Bogotá.

In Santafé de Bogotá, the name of LAS CUATRO ESTACIONES is a symbol of refinement, excellence and good taste in food.

The pleasure of trying the meats of the CUATRO ESTACIONES and enjoy its carefull service in an ambience of elegance.

A meeting of friends, a celebration or a business meeting which takes place there, becomes an unforgettable experience.

The menu, comprising a variety of dishes from different countries, is the result of professionalism for several decades, which today facilitates anticipating the wishes of a diversity of personalities and world cultures.

LAS CUATRO ESTACIONES' fame is not only a local phenomenon: it has crossed borders, as the different international prizes with which the restaurant has been awarded testify.

It would be a loss if during your next visit to Santafé de Bogotá you did not program time to enjoy the magic of LAS CUATRO ESTACIONES.

The city has a lively night life; a multitude of events are programmed daily in which both national and international artists perform, and among many options the possibility of enjoying an exquisite dinner in one of its magnificent restaurants and enjoy a «night out on the town» in one of its discoteques.

On this page, a night scene of Bogotá and the Ballet de Colombia, one of the folklore groups which best represent the dances and traditions of Colombia.

"The Universidad de La Sabana does not just seek academic excellence; since its founding it understands that the goal of the University lies in human perfection, integral education, and full academic, spiritual, cultural and sports development.

In La Sabana the person comes first, the person who transcends with his work, with research, Man in search of truth."

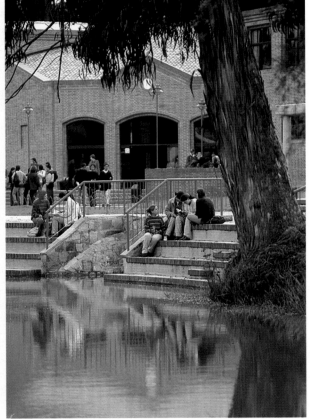

The Escuela Colombiana de Ingeniería Julio Garavito (Colombian School of Engineering) combines the dynamic and rapid growth of a relatively young university with the composure of principles and academic and scientific fundamentals which assure it soundness and permanence.

On October 20, 1972, a group of visionary engineers and engineering professors gave birth to the Colombian School of Engineering for the purpose of training professionals with an excellent technical preparation and great sense of social solidarity. This requires an integral education involving as much scientific and technical aspects as humanistic and social ones, and enshrines the principle of non-discrimination on political, religious, ethnic or social grounds.

Its immense rural area covers 70 acres, located at Kilometer 13 along Bogotá's northern trunk road, and its comfortable facilities provide a beautiful natural ambience for over 4.000 undergraduate and graduate students.

The School has five engineering programs - civil, electrical, electronic, and industrial engineering, and information science - and a program in

economics, set up in response to a survey of the development needs of Colombian society. With a firm step, specialized engineering in the areas of structures, hydraulics and environmental control have been initiated. International exchange and cooperation agrreements are made with universities in Europe and North America.

Teaching takes place in the School, where research, teaching, further education and external services take place, and knowledge is disseminated by means of the institution's magazine, books, manuals, notes, and essays. With the progress in computing and telecommunications, these groups are networked to the rest of the world.

In 1970 the government granted the family compensation funds the faculty to invest in social development programs which contribute to improve the living conditions of workers and their families. As a result, CAFAM put the Melgar Vacation Center into service, an original recreational complex, unique of its kind in South America.

65 miles from Santafé de Bogotá and at 1.400 ft. above sea-level, and with a temperature of 81oF, it has 354 huts in which 3.160 people can relax, each of which has complete services. These facilities are complemented with the Hotel Almirante which is located in the Vacation Center. It has a capacity for 220 people in 61 rooms and an area designed for business events.

These services are complemented with broad facilities for recreation which allow children and adults to enjoy training and diversion at all hours. A supermarket facilitates visitors' purchases and during the off-peak season CAFAM offers attractive plans.

In 1995 CAFAM opened the Kualamaná Convention Center and Resort, which has a capacity to lodge 532 people in 154 rooms.

The companies affiliated to CAFAM can make use of a convention center designed with the necessary technology for conferences, congresses and conventions, and the best bar and restaurant facilities, sports and recreation, thus enabling the businessman to also enjoy relaxation and rest.

There are many reasons why the Melgar Vacation Center is a special place for promoting a united family, in a healthy environment which provides for recreation and relaxation.

Kualamaná Convention Center & Resort

Lake at Melgar Vacation Center

The UNIVERSIDAD EL BOSQUE, previously the ESCUELA COLOMBIANA DE MEDICINA, founded in 1977, commenced work with the Faculty of Medicine on Febuary 12, 1979. Today, transformed into the Universidad El Bosque, since Febuary 5, 1997, it has several undergraduate and postgraduate programs. It is a private, non-profit higher-education institution, whose mission is to contribute to the development of Colombian society through educational programs at university level. Its historical site is the Ranch and the meaning of its logo is the representation of the snakes as the mythological animals of pre-Columbian Chibcha Indian medicine. Its motto: "For a culture of life, its quality and meaning".

In the Cundinamarca countryside life of small farmers remains as peaceful and quiet as in the times of the Spanish Colony.

Below, the Nemocón Valley surroundings. From this mountains the Muisca indians extracted the salt they exchanged for gold to make their ritual ornaments.

The plains of Bogotá produce the most beautiful flowers in the world and around and about the city there are villages which continue to preserve old traditions, among them, the making of pottery vessels, virgin wool blankets and basket-weaving.
Page 129, Neusa Reservoir is one of the most peaceful spots on the plains; here you can do watersports and camp in the park surrounded by a pine forest.

BOYACÁ

To the north-east of the plains of Bogotá lie the fertile soils of the state of Boyacá. It has peaceful and serene countryside in the high, cold part of the Eastern Cordillera, where small villages preserve their traditions and country life.

The eastern part of the state extends to the foothills of the *cordillera*, which mark the boundary with the vast grassland plains of the state of Casanare, and the western part descends to a narrow strip which ends in the hot depression of the lower Magdalena Valley. To the north, a huge mountain range opens up, extending to the Chicamocha Gorge and the Sierra Nevada del Cocuy. Boyacá also has desert-like areas, large lakes and thermal springs, Pisba National Nature Park, El Cocuy National Nature Park and Iguaque Sanctuary of Flora and Fauna.

The population of Boyacá is basically rural: 55% inhabit and work in the countryside and grow mainly potato, wheat, barley and other cereal crops, market vegetables and fruits. On the high ground dairying predominates. The state also has important mines such as the Paz del Río steelworks and the emerald mines in the Muzo area, where the most beautiful emeralds in the world are found.

Boyacá has a long-standing tradition of crafts. Country folk from the different regions supplement their income by making and selling all kinds of crafts. Textiles include garments made from wool dyed with bright colors, which are made in Sogamoso, Chiquinquirá and Paipa, among other towns. Blankets, especially those from Nobsa, are woven from white virgin wool, which is spun on a spindle. Ponchos, the traditional wear of Colombian country folk, are made in Iza, Cocuy and Sogamoso. The sculpting of the ivory palm nut, or *tagua*, is famous in Tinjacá. Pottery, an art inherited by the inhabitants from their Indian ancestors, is made in the village of Ráquira and its environs.

The countryside of Boyacá was the setting for the battles which sealed independence for Colombia: at the Pantano de Vargas and the Puente de Boyacá, the troops led by Bolívar and Santander vanquished the pacifying army and

Doorway of the La Candelaria Monastery near Ráquira.

Page 132, due to the importance which Tunja attained during the Colony and the need evangelize the Indians, churches were built whose magnificence continues to impress. Facade of the San Agustín Convent.

Page 133, Iza was chosen as the prettiest village in Boyacá for the care with which its inhabitants have preserved its buildings; detail of a house on the plaza.

put an end to the dominion of Ferdinand VII of Spain over these territories. Both spots pay homage to the struggle for national liberation: at the Pantano de Vargas stands the monument «Homage to the Lancers of the LLano», the work of sculptor Rodrigo Arenas Betancourt.

TUNJA

The state capital, Tunja is situated on a terrace in the highland area of Boyacá, at 10.000 ft. above sea-level and with a mean temperature of 48°F. It was founded in 1539 by Gonzalo Suárez Rendón on the spot which had been the seat of the *cacicazgo* of Hunza. It soon became a cultural center and place of residence for important inhabitants of the region. It was the provincial capital and in 1812 the seat of Congress of the United Provinces of Nueva Granada. In 1816 the town was occupied by Pablo Morillo's troops, and the battles which put an end to Spanish dominion were fought nearby, for which reason Simón Bolívar dubbed the town «Birthplace and workshop of liberty». It was a obligatory stopping place on the road to Cartagena and Caracas, the city which long vied with Bogotá for supremacy.

The colonial architecture which typifies the city, partly sixteenth century, is one of the richest and most beautiful that this era left as a heritage in Nueva Granada. The churches and convents are not only notable for their architecture, but also for the extraordinary decoration and for the woodcarvings and paintings by the most important painters of colonial centuries, such as Angélico Medoro, Gregorio Vásquez Ceballos and the Figueroa brothers. Noteworthy are the Cathedral, the churches of San Francisco, Santo Domingo (with its marvellous Rosary Chapel), and Santa Bárbara, and the chapels of El Topo, Santa Clara and Las Nieves. Examples of civil architecture include the house of the Founder on the Plaza Mayor and the house of the scribe Juan de Vargas - with their extraordinary, well-preserved murals and other paintings - today the seats of clubs, hotels and government institutions.

VILLAGES OF BOYACÁ

Villa de Leyva·was founded in 1572 by Andrés Díaz Venero de Leyva, the first president of the Nuevo Reino de Granada. Surrounding its large cobbled square stand the church and colonial houses such as that of *los portales* where Don Juan de Castellanos wrote his «Elegies to Illustrious Men of the Indies» and those of the Town Council and Congress. From its begin-

nings the village was a resting place for travelers and government officials and it was here that the hero of national independence, Antonio Nariño, spent his last days. Its colonial architecture is outstanding: noteworthy are the monasteries both in the village and around about, also the little squares, the cobbled streets and the mills which today have been turned into hotels. The paleontology museum holds a magnificent collection of fossils, witness to a remote past when the region formed part of the seabed. Near Villa de Leyva important vestiges of ancient fossils are found; also the remains of Indian culture such as El Infiernillo, a pre-Columbian astronomical observatory and ceremonial site, and Iguaque Lake where, according to Muiska tradition, Mankind originated: the goddess Bachué and her son emerged from the lake and after having peopled these lands, turned into serpents and slipped back into the water.

In the plaza of Sáchica, a nearby village, scenes from Christ's Passion are reenacted during Holy Week. Other beautiful and peaceful spots are Ráquira, a charming population famous for its pottery going back to colonial times, Tópaga and Monguí. They are, as with the majority of the villages of Boyacá, true colonial jewels for their churches and plazas, their streets and houses.

Paipa and its surroundings possess an important tourist complex which in addition to excellent hotels, is famous for its thermal baths. Duitama and Sogamoso are active towns which link agriculture and dairying to the center of the state and to the Llanos region. The little villages lining the roads are true relics of a past rich in woollen crafts, basket-weaving, pottery and also in very old traditions and legends which continue to endure. The town of Chiquinquirá is a place of pilgrimage because it is where, since the sixteenth century, the miraculous image of the Virgin of the Rosary of Chiquinquirá has been venerated, in whose honor the great cathedral was built. The cathedral preserves the image, which was originally painted on a coarse canvas by village craftsmen, and which after having deteriorated and almost completely fallen to pieces miraculously became restored. Since then it is venerated as the patron saint of Colombia and when Pope John Paul II visited the country he renewed such worship.

One of the major attractions of the area is Tota Lake, where you can go sailing, take a trip by launch, or do watersports. There are comfortable hotels and stopping places on its banks, where you can enjoy a pleasant atmosphere.

*Page 134, the house of the founder of the city, Gonzalo Suárez Rendón, next to the
catherdral, has the basic layout of an Andalusian house with a wide hallway and patio
flanked by a cloister of arches and columns; inside there are a series of magnificent murals.*

*Page 135, panorama of Tunja's Plaza de Bolívar and the Chapel of the Rosary in the church
of Santo Domingo, the most imposing expression of American baroque in Colombia.*

In 1996 the Principal's Office committed itself to taking the University to many regions of the country. This purpose has been put into practice with an admirable tenacity. That very same year the University opened its doors in Tunja, in the building that for many years was home to the Santo Domingo School, one of the best schools of Boyacá. In ample, comfortable and appropriate facilities, the students receive a humane and professional education that prepares them to face the challenges that the personal, social and regional development will present them. It is not an exaggeration to say that the Santo Tomás University promotes the progress of Boyacá.

Beside the basilica of Our Lady of the Rosary stands the Universidad Santo Tomás branch in the town of Chiquinquirá, in western Boyacá. Offering two programs (Psychology and Economy and Business Administration), and as an open university 7 degrees, 4 technical professional courses and 4 postgraduate degrees in education, the University opened it classrooms on August 15, 1997. This evidently benefits the people of the south of the state of Santander, western Boyacá and the north of Cundinamarca. It corroborates the irreversible direction which the regionalization of the University has taken.

During the Colony, Villa de Leyva was a resting place for travelers and officials of the viceroyship. It has become an attractive tourist center where different activities are held: horse racing, religious festivals in honor of the Virgin of Chinquinquirá and San Isidro, and important events such as the Kite Festival in August.

There are beautiful and peaceful places in the state of Boyacá which offer rest and seclusion,
such as Tota Lake, where you can also do diverse watersports,
go sailing and fish for rainbow trout.

Around Sochagota Lake, near the town of Paipa, there are magnificent hotels,
thermal baths and a large convention center.

In every corner of Boyacá there are lively and surprising contrasts; economic activity ranges
from the steel industry of Paz del Río to the delicate craftwork in the Tenza Valley.
The whiteness of the walls with which the Colony illuminated Sáchica Church
and the lively indigenous color of the houses in Ráquira,
make the state one of the most diverse in the country.

THE SANTANDER STATES

The states of Santander and Norte de Santander lie to the north-east of Colombia, and border with Venezuela. The region, lying mostly in the Eastern Cordillera, is one of the most mountainous in the country and enjoys the natural advantages which the different climatic zones provide, from the tropical rain forest of Magdalena Medio, to the climate of the páramos which are found in the eastern part of the state of Santander. Historically this region has been very important for having been an obligatory passing point on the route to the Caribbean and Venezuela, and during the past century for being where foreign immigrants settled, mainly Germans, who gave impetus to the development of the region.

During the eighteenth century, the region which is today the state of Santander, was the most important crafts manufacturing center of the economy of Nueva Granada. The region produced blankets, linen, tobacco, and hats and supplied a good part of the country with its products. Socorro, in 1781, the year of the rising of the comuneros, had over 14.000 inhabitants, while Tunja barely passed 3.000. Crafts manufacture concentrated workers in villages and villas, which was a phe-

nomenal exception at that time with respect to the rest of the country, where the village, town or villa was just a market center. In 1857, according to writer Anibal Galindo, there were 7.132 manufacturers in Santander, while in Antioquia there were only 2.

Another relevant aspect of the industrialization of the region of Santander was the appearance of an oil enclave at Barrancabermeja, which together with Bucaramanga formed the poles of development around which the regional economy gravitated. Barrancabermeja became an oil production and refining center at the beginning of the twentieth century.

This novel element in the region, oil, appeared just at the moment at which the rigor of the coffee crisis in Santander began to be felt. Up until then, the region had supplied 30% of the coffee which Colombia exported to international markets. The economic relief for Santander which the oil industry provided permitted the region to maintain its standard of living and growth, to the point that Bucaramanga is the fifth city in industrial and commercial importance in Colombia and the unquestionable pole of development for the region of Santander.

Page 142, street in the town of Socorro.

Page 143, house in Barichara.

SANTANDER

The state of Santander is one of the most rugged areas of the country. A good part of the region lies in the Eastern Cordillera, deeply cut by the Chicamocha, Suárez and Fonce rivers. The remaining area is located in the middle valley of the Magadalena River. Rainfall is very varied in Santander, where there are very dry areas, such as the Chicamocha Gorge where annual rainfall is below 500 mm, and very humid areas such as some parts of the Magdalena Medio valley, which receives 3.800 mm annually.

BUCARAMANGA

The city of Bucaramanga was founded in 1622 by Andrés Pérez de Sotomayor, in what were the lands of cacique Bucarica. Known as the «City of Parks», Bucaramanga is situated at 3.000 ft. above sea-level on an inclined terrace of the Eastern Cordillera and has a mean temperature of 73oF. Industry, commerce and services are the main sources of income of the district of Bucaramanga.

The educational and cultural life of Bucaramanga is also important, since it has excellent high schools, commercial and industrial schools, and universities of national standing such as the Universidad Industrial de Santander.

Bucaramanga possesses an important hotel infrastructure, and events which take place periodically include the Feria Bonita, the Luis A. Calvo Festival of Colombian Andean Music, the International Piano festival, the Marionette Festival and the National Week of the Tiple.

Girón lies within the metropolitan area of Bucaramanga, a beautiful village founded in 1631 by Francisco Mantilla on the banks of the Golden River. The main economic activities of the region are based on agriculture and mining, which in the past made possible the development of a wonderful colonial architecture, well maintained, such as the Religious Art Museum in the central park.

Socorro, situated in the north-east of the state, is a territory with a glorious past, the birthplace of the comuneros and of great deeds in the epic emancipation. In 1781 Manuela Beltrán tore down an edict that increased taxes and contributions, which resulted in the Rebellion of the Comuneros. In the main square of Socorro, in addition to its imposing cathedral of carved stone, there are monuments to the leaders of the comuneros, José Antonio Galán and Antonia Santos.

Page 144, El Gallineral Park in San Gil, one of the most beautiful and peaceful spots in the region of Santander, is situated on a small island on the Fonce River and owes its name to a special kind of moss which hangs from the trees in the form of a long, thick beard.

Page 145, country folk of Santander in Confines, a village in Comunera Province.

Another important settlement is Barichara, a charming village declared a National Monument because of its colonial architecture and its streets of large stone slabs.

NORTE DE SANTANDER

In the state of Norte de Santander there are three geographical zones: the first is the hill range of the Motilones, on whose slopes some villages are situated and on whose peaks, covered in jungle, several Indian tribes live, and from where the rivers which run towards Lake Maracaibo in Venezuela rise; the second comprises the branch of the cordillera which separates from the Santurbán Knot and runs for a short while through the state before entering Venezuelan territory; and the third corresponds to the slopes and valley of Catatumbo, in the middle of the two branches of the cordi-llera, which has as its center Lake Maracaibo, a region of high humidity, heavy rainfall and a sparse population.

Agriculture is Norte de Santander's main economic activity, where coffee, corn, yucca, sugar-cane, beans, plantain and African palm are well developed on the slopes of the cordillera. In the high parts potato, barley, wheat, vegetable and fruits are grown. Cat-

tle ranching is a good complement to the region's economy. Oil fields are exploited in the region of Catatumbo and in the valley of the Zulia River. This region has close economic ties with Venezuela.

CÚCUTA

The state capital, Cúcuta is situated in the valley of the Zulia River at a fork in the Eastern Cordillera, which continues on towards Venezuela to the east and towards the peninsula of La Guajira to the north.

In 1875 Cúcuta was destroyed by an earthquake, and after being rebuilt it was besieged and destroyed once again in 1900 during the Thousand Days War. Today it is an active center of border trade with Venezuela. The economy, as in any border town, has suffered from the instability of foreign exchange fluctuations between the Colombian peso and Venezuelan bolívar, altering, according to the true rate, the political climate and bilateral relations. Nevertheless, there is a constant influx of visitors and the city maintains its commercial vitality. It shares the benefits of this interchange with San Antonio del Táchira, in Venezuela.

Page 146, Bucaramanga, the city of parks, has such beautiful and traditional spots
as the cathedral of the Sagrada Familia, situated in Santander Park.

Page 147, House of Luis Perú de la Croix, Simón Bolívar's aide-de-camp,
from whose inner courtyard the towers of the church of San Laureano can be seen.

The Soto Club, founded in 1873, became years later the Commerce Club,
whose present-day home dates from 1922.

The village of Girón, within the metropolitan area of Bucaramanga, stands on the banks of the Golden River; it was declared a national monument for its beautiful colonial buildings, the cathedral of Barichara, one of the most beautiful and best preserved villages in Colombia, has a sober facade notable for its magnificent stone work

The village of Santa Cruz and San Gil of the Nueva Baeza, called the pearl of the Fonce River, was founded in 1689 and today is the third biggest town in the state and Confines, a beautiful village hidden in the cordillera, is one of the most remote of the state; its church was declared a national monument.

In 1973 the Santo Tomás University opened a center in Bucaramanga, the beautiful and prosperous capital of Santander. Soon it became one of the most prestigious institutions of higher education in the eastern region of Colombia. Young students from Santander, Norte de Santander, Boyacá and Cesar come to this campus. Once they become professionals, and responding to the education they received, they devote themselves to the development of their regions. It is not a coincidence that since the Bucaramanga center started operating, this city has experienced an unparalleled progress. The Santo Tomás University at Bucaramanga offers eleven undergraduate programs and sixteen postgraduate certificate programs, seven of them through the distance education service.

Vélez was the first urban settlement founded by the Spanish in Santander,
in the year 1539; it is today the principal producer of bocadillo,
the most typical foodstuff of the region, made from guava.

The state of Santander has places of great beauty such as the Afrodita Cascade near San Gil.

In the Villa del Rosario, near Cúcuta, the Templo is preserved, an historic place in whose sacristy the first Contitutional Congress of Colombia was held in 1821; it is situated on the plaza of Los Mártires, where many patriots were shot during the reign of terror of Pablo Morillo's pacification campaign.

THE CARIBBEAN REGION

The Colombian Caribbean coast cover an area of nearly 50.000 sq. miles, with an island area of 17.800 sq. miles. Its main geographical areas are the peninsula of La Guajira, the Sierra Nevada de Santa Marta, the delta of the Magdalena River, the plains of the hinterland, the valleys of the Sinú and San Jorge rivers, the Mompox depression, the Urabá region and the archipelago of San Andrés and Old Providence. It is conformed by the mainland states of La Guajira, Magdalena, Cesar, Bolívar, Sucre, and Córdoba, and by the islands of San Andrés and Old Providence.

With the arrival of the Spanish, the plains of the Colombian Caribbean were inhabited by Indian tribes which had reached a high cultural level. One of these tribes, the Zenú Indians, had built on the flood plain of the San Jorge River a network of drainage channels which covered an area of 2.000 sq. miles. They were peaceful communities but their riches, especially their funerary offerings, awoke Spanish greed. The communities were practically annihilated and

The «sea of seven colors» of San Andrés Island.

during the seventeenth century the survivors became dispersed.

Another culture, the Tayrona Indians, built a complex network of towns connected by stone paths in the Sierra Nevada de Santa Marta. Their descendents still inhabit the high peaks.

The Caribbean region was the first region to be populated in prehistoric times, and the first to be explored by the Europeans of the Rennaissance. The extinct Santa María la Antigua del Darién has the privilege to be the oldest of the settlements founded by the Spanish in Colombian territory (1510), and the birthplace of the literature of the New World, since it was there that the first chronicles which discovered the new continent were written, to the wonder of Europe. The towns of Santa Marta (1525), Cartagena (1533), Riohacha (1545), the Villa of Tolú (1535) and the river port of Mompox (1540), permitted organizing, at the dawn of the Colony, the exploration of the interior of the country, once the Conquest of the Indians had been con-

solidated. The strategic position of the Colombian Caribbean ports explains the richness of their architecture and urban layout, especially Cartagena. The region has continued to grow in importance, since the Caribbean basin today achieves the true integration of the three Americas.

The present-day population of the Caribbean coast is the result of the *mestizaje* of three ethnic groups over several centuries: the Spanish, Indians and finally the Negroes who replaced the Indians in the sugar mills and in the fields of the haciendas.

During the sixteenth and seventeenth centuries, Indian and negro slaves escaped to set up *palenques*, villages of runaway slaves. Over time these palenques became so powerful that around the year 1620 they had a population of 20.000 inhabitants, protected by stockades, pits and traps.

The process of mestizaje accelerated with the appearance of the haciendas, where «free» workers were hired for agricultural work. The new labor force set up

near the haciendas or on the lands of their «master».

Together with racial mestizaje, cultural mestizaje also took place. . The axe and hatchet, together with the match and the flint, were added to the Indian custom of felling and burning, and accelerated the destruction of the forests, for the purpose of incorporating new lands within the agricultural frontier. Traditional cuisine was revolutionized with the introduction of plantain from Asia, sugar-cane, rice, yucca and citric fruits, among other products. Cattle also adapted to the new environment and prospered. The incorporation of iron in the manufacture of tools resulted in an increase in the efficiency of work. The Spanish Catholic religion replaced the myths and beliefs of the Indians and African slaves, and native and negro liturgies intermingled with Christian dogmas and rites.

Negro and Indian music and songs were incorporated into rituals and fiestas. African drums were the basis of the *vallenato* drum of the states of Cesar, Magdalena and La Guajira; flutes and pipes used by the Indians were incorporated into the vernacular music of the Caribbean, enriched by the contribution of the guitar, tambourine and accordion from Europe. With respect to the origins of the music of the Caribbean coast, researchers agree that it is the result of the mix of European and native aires with the latter, in which African music dominates. Examples of this process of musical mestizaje include the *cumbia*, *puya* or *porro tapao*, *zafra*, *paseo*, *son vallenato* and *merengue*.

In the saga of the Buendía family - the central characters of 'One Hundred Years of Solitude', by Gabriel Garía Márquez - which circled the globe and earned Colombia the very name of Macondo. The paintings of Alejandro Obregón or Enrique Grau, the vallenato of Alejo Durán or Rafael Escalona, are a national heritage which projects the country's best image to the rest of the world. But the creativity of the people of the Caribbean coast is also portrayed in a religious syncretism its popular myths, its dances and fiestas which are displayed with such vivaciousness and gaiety in all its celebrations and especially at carnival time.

CARTAGENA DE INDIAS

Situated on one of the most beautiful bays in Latin America, Cartagena de Indias, capital of the state of Bolívar, was since its founding in 1533 by Don Pedro de Heredia, the most important port of the vast Spanish colonial empire in America, and for this reason, the most coveted prize by pirates and corsairs. And by England and France, which rivalled Spain for world supremacy.

Thanks to the privileged conditions of the area —a natural bay surrounded by navigation channels, islands, ciénagas and lagoons which are among the largest and safest in the world— Cartagena very soon began to acquire importance as a seaport and a departure point for penetrating inland into the territory.

From 1556 on, the Spanish authorities commenced the complex task of protecting the town with stockades against possible attacks by the Indians, and subsequently with the largest and most important ring of defenses of any settlement in the New World. To surround the town they built walls and bastions such as Santa Catalina, San Lucas, Santiago y San Pedro, until the nucleus of the town was well protected. The wall was later extended to cover the slum quarter of Getsemaní.

Thus the most imposing castle that the Spanish were to build in the Nuevo Reino took shape: San Felipe de Barajas, on Lázaro hill, the all-time masterwork of military engineering. This fortress played a key role when the English admiral Sir Edward Vernon attacked the town in 1741. Around the second half of the seventeenth century Cartagena was to earn the fame of being an «impregnable» city.

The old city, enclosed by the walls and bastions which have earned it the name of «stone corral», is architecturally homogenous and exceptionally beautiful, in which the majority of the buildings reflect their Andalucian heritage, with a central patio and abundant vegetation, surrounded by arches and columns and on the outside pretty doorways and overhanging balconies, which create a special atmosphere. To walk down the streets with their romantic names is to regress to the living past to discover squares, churches, convents, and enormous town houses.

Thanks to this important colonial heritage, Cartagena de Indias was named Historical Heritage of Mankind in 1984, being the first place in Colombia to enter the List of Cultural and Natural World Heritage, under the designation «Port, Fort and Monumental Ensemble of Cartagena».

Outside the walled city, the bustle of a modern city is once again felt, with its commerce, industry and, of course, its tourist spots, which seasonally attract thousands of visitors to the beaches of El Laguito, Bocagrande and Marbella, lined by imposing hotels and restaurants.

But it is not only tourism which enlivens Cartagena. Its modern and spacious Convention Center, its magnificent hotels, its important industrial zone and its traditional charm, has made it an obligatory place for all kinds of national and international congresses and conferences, and for organizing a multitude of events, from the popular National Beauty Contest, to film festivals and Caribbean music.

Leaving the city, the peninsula of Barú is situated to the south of Cartagena, with splendid beaches and recreational and hotel facilities. 28 miles to the south-west and a couple of hours by launch lie the Rosary Islands, an archipelago of coral and transparent waters, ideal for relaxation and snorkelling.

During the reign of Felipe II, the Spanish Crown decided to surround Cartagena de Indias
with walls, castles and bastions, in order to protect it from attack by its enemies who
harrassed the settlement, hoping to sack it for its riches.

On the opposite page, the Castle of San Felipe de Barajas, the greatest work of military
architecture undertaken by the Spanish in South America.

On this page: the fort of San Fernando, situated in Bocachica;
the bastion of Santa Catalina, in the walled city.

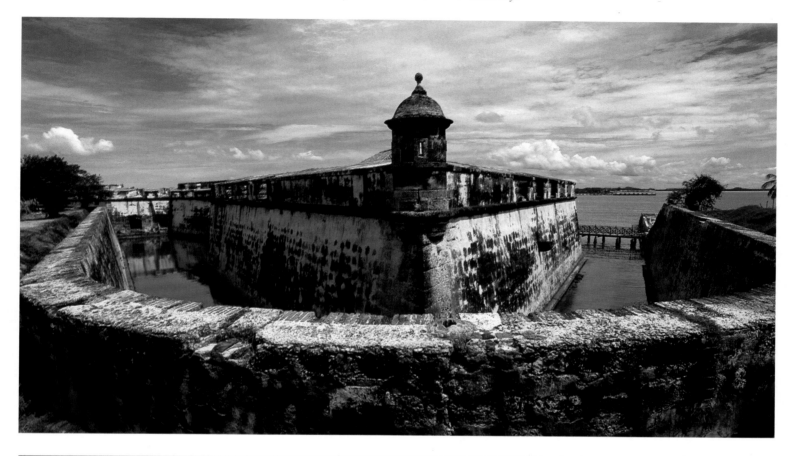

Within the walled city the other Cartagena is found, that of squares, churches, narrow streets
and balconies which give the city a pleasant and intimate atmosphere.

Above, the Calle de la Iglesia; the cathedral tower can be seen in the background.

Tower of the church of Santo Domingo, the oldest in the city.

Below, night view of the Plaza de la Aduana, from the town hall.

Panorama of the Bóveda, which were prison cells during the Colony;
today craft shops function there.

Above, the Clock Tower, built mid-nineteenth century over the Boca del Puente which gave access to the walled city. The house-museum of Rafael Núñez - situated in the barrio of Cabrero - illustrious stateman, President of the Republic, promoter of the Constitution of 1886 and author of the lyrics of the National Anthem.

Below, the Portal de los Dulces, opposite the Plaza de los Coches, and the Santa Clara Convent, today converted into a magnificent hotel.

This is Banco Superior - Diners Club, leader in Colombia. In Cartagena, historical heritage of Mankind, the Bank contributed with the restoration of republican buildings at its main office located in the Getsemaní neighborhood. In the city our members also have three more offices at their disposal in the Paseo de la Castellana, Bocagrande and the San Diego neighborhood.

Cartagena de Indias in not only walls and colonial houses. There are also peaceful neighborhoods of Republican architecture and tall buildings where modern life takes place.

Top: Manga, one of the most exclusive and traditional areas in Cartagena.

Bottom: Buildings in El Laguito.

Cartagena also is a modern city with hotels, shopping malls, beaches and recreational spots, which are on a par with the great cities of the world.

On this page, panorama of El Laguito, where a large part of tourism is concentrated, and the Aquarium on the island of San Martín de Pajarales, in the archipelago of Nuestra Señore del Rosario, now a National Nature Park.

On the following page, the marinas opposite the Club de Pesca, where sailing vessels from all over the world tie up.

SANTA CRUZ DE MOMPOX

On the banks of the Magdalena River, 154 miles south of Cagrtaena and also in the state of Bolívar, amidst lush grasslando plains surrounded by ciénagas, lies Santa Cruz de Mompox, one of the Conony_ most beautiful architectural jewels. Founded in 1540 on one of the few natural elevations of the region, a former settlement of the Malibú Indians, it rapidly became an important port and trading route for the transport of merchandise and travellers between Cartagena and inland regions.

Owing to the fact that the region was not suitable for large-scale agriculture, the town depended basically on river trade, thanks to its intermediate location in the vast coastal region of northern Colombia. In the 18th century the river changed its course and on becoming isolated, the town lost its importance as a river port. It was precisely thanks to this isolation that Mompox has remained almost intact up until the present day.

In addition to fulfilling their missionary and doctrinal functions, the Franciscans, Dominicans, Jesuits and Agustinians helped maintain order and subject the Indians to the Spanish Crown. In Mompox, as in the majority of the towns of the New World, social organization arose from from religious needs and urban development hinged on the churches, where the creativity and orginality of their buildings, and the rich and varied ornamentation which were mixed with elements brought from Europe, together with the creative contribution of the Indians, were wonderfully incorporated. On its streets, important civil buildings alternate with religious ones, located in the different squares, which make this tropical village so charming, well-known for its Holy Week celebrations, among others.

In recognition of such a pure example of colonial architecture, Mompox was declared a National Monument in 1959, and in 1995 was included in the World Heritage of Mankind by UNESCO.

Page 168, Street in Santa Cruz de Mompox.

Page 169, Santa Bárbara Church

BARRANQUILLA

What gave Barranquilla its importance and distinctive character was its strategic location on the mouth of the Magdalena River. Since the middle of the past century when railway lines were laid to link production centers with the river and a strong impetus was given to steamship navigation, Barranquilla enjoyed rapid progress, attracting people from all over the country and becoming an ever more populous, attractive and important city.

Historical circumstances favored the development of Barranquilla during this century and gave it one of its distinguishing marks. Pioneers from abroad, especially Germans, North Americans, and immigrants from the Near and Middle East, not only found a favorable place for the development of all kinds of industrial and commercial initiatives but found in the inhabitant of Barranquilla the perfect complement for their projects. Thus, with foreign capi-

tal and expertise and local innovative spirit, many companies prospered at a very fast pace. For this reason, many foreign colonies are found in Barranquilla which have become Colombian in their customs and have involved the local culture in their gastronomic and architectural prefernces, to mention only a couple of examples. Barranquilla's development stimulated interest in training its inhabitants, and there are a number of higher educational facilities which have permitted the city to consolidate its prestige as a cultural city, in addition to its importance as a commercial and industrial center.

During the present century the growth and modernization of Barranquilla have been impressive. In 1920 the Parrish brothers, in association with local investors, set up the Compañía Urbanizadora El Prado, and conceived a neighborhood which was to become an urban innovation in Colombia. In an area covering 740 acres, the

Page 170, «Miss Universe» building in the business center of the city.

Page 171, House in the barrio of El Prado.

On this page, the Barranquilla Carnival takes place during the four days before Ash Wednesday. Carnival floats and dancers parade down the streets in an outburst of revelry which has made it the most important fiesta on the Caribbean coast.

urban development of El Prado commenced, which for the time was larger than many urban settlements in the country. The idea was to develop a neighborhood on the outskirts of the city in the style of a North American suburb. Subsequently the neighborhood was complemented with a Country Club and a luxury hotel. El Prado thus became the first neighborhood to have complete public services, such as electricity in the home, street lighting, water supply and drainage, telephones, street cleaning and trash collection. The example of Barranquilla was soon to be imitated in other Colombian towns. This growth and modernization has not ceased, and for this reason Barranquilla today has top-quality, modern architecture and a hotel infrastructure in accordance with its standing as a port of international trade, offering the visitor all the conveniences of a metropolis.

In addition, Barranquilla soon became notable as a cultural city, irradiating its influence along the Caribbean coast. By 1920 a group of intellectuals had emerged, led by José Feliz Fuenmayor and Ramón Vinyes, a Catalonian from Spain who had a book business which published the magazine 'Voces', one of the most pioneering avant garde magazines that have existed in Colombia. The Barranquilla Group as it came to be known, had a profound effect on the social environment, so much so that it can be said that from it emerged the literary art of Gabriel García Márquez, Alvaro Cepeda Samudio, Fuenmayor, and Héctor Rojas Herazo; the painting of Alejandro Obregón, Cecilia Porras and Noé León; the photography of Nereo, and much other talent.

One of the important attractions of «the golden gate of Colombia», as Barranquilla is known, is the famous Carnival, which takes place from the 20th of January and which has been celebrated for over a century. The Carnival has become a part of the city's character and reveals the warmth, emotiveness and exuberance of the Caribbean personality.

Panorama of Barranquilla with the Hotel El Prado, one of the most traditional in the city, in the foreground and the Terminal Marítimo y Fluvial, situated on the west bank of the Magdalena river and endowed with an excellent infrastructure and equipment.

Below, Puerto Colombia lies just nine miles from Barranquilla, with attractive beaches and the old Quay, built between 1888 and 1893 and the Ciénaga Grande de Santa Marta, the largest natural lake in Colombia. Two fishermen's villages are found in the Ciénaga.

Today, Barranquilla is the fourth city in the country and an outstanding cultural and business center.

Top: The Amira de la Rosa theater

Bottom: Panoramic view of the city.

On the corner of calle 76 with carrera 58 a building was constructed exclusively for the headquarters of the Banco Superior in Barranquilla, the city where the members of this institution have five offices at their disposal, and where a complete portfolio of products and services to cover their financial needs is available.

Santa Marta

Founded in 1525 by Rodrigo de Bastidas, Santa Marta is the oldest surviving town built by the Spanish in Colombia, and the present-day capital of the state of Magdalena. Its location was chosen for the beauty and security of its imposing bay, and it was from here that the conquest of the Nuevo Reino de Granada commenced. Although Santa Marta was supplanted by Cartagena as the main port on the Caribbean during the Colony, it was the capital of a governance and as such developed an important architecture - although less so than in Cartagena. Nevertheless, Santa Marta has sufficient natural resources to be attractive for both national and international tourism. The neighboring area of Tayrona Park, charming fishing villages such as Taganga, and the proximity of the Sierra Nevada de Santa Marta, in addition to its excellent beaches, make Santa Marta a notable spot on the Colombian Caribbean coast.

At the beginning of the present century, Santa Marta suffered an abrupt change in its development as a result of the arrival of North American companies which set up plantations for the export of bananas, on which the region's economy came to depend, and which resulted in the disturbances and revolts characteristic of a process of adaptation to the industrial era. In recent times the tourist sector has been strengthened, since the city has undeniable advantages over other coastal cities.

Tayrona National Park is without doubt the most important tourist resource in the area. Situated east of Taganga, it covers an area of 58 sq. miles: 46 sq. miles is land and 12 sq. miles coastal water.

Sierra Nevada de Santa Marta

The Sierra Nevada de Santa Marta is a mountainous massif independent of the Andean system, which rises from sea-level to 20.670 ft., covering all the climatic zones produced by the topography. The mountain spurs are the habitat of three different Indian tribes: Kogi, Ika and Sanha, and also settlers who have come to live on these slopes in recent years. There are two urban settlements of the Tayrona cultura: Pueblito and Ciudad Perdida.

Buritaca 200 or Ciudad Perdida, a complex of paved terraces and paths which link villages together, retaining walls, wells, water tanks, and canals to regulate the courses of rivers and streams, is the result of a profound knowledge of engineering and agriculture which the Tayrona Indians had developed. There are remains of over 200 urban settlements of this pre-Hispanic culture which had been covered for centuries by the jungle.

Santa Marta Cathedral.

Santa Marta is the oldest town in Colombia. It was founded by Rodrigo de Bastidas in 1525, in one of the most beautiful bays in the Caribbean and at the foot of the Sierra Nevada de Santa Marta. Monument to its founder in the legendary Paseo Bastidas.

The Quinta de San Pedro Alejandrino, built in the sixteenth century in Mediterranean style, was the place which gave refuge to Simón Bolívar when he was on his way into exile; he died there on December 17, 1830. The hacienda preserves the old installations, sugar mills, distilleries, stables and innumerable momentos of the Liberator.

Recently the Bolivarian Museum was built on the grounds.

The El Rodadero tourist complex (above), located on the bay of Gaira, one of the most
attractive tourist centers of the Caribbean, has excellent hotels,
restaurants, casinos and discoteques.

Taganga (below), a hospitable fishermen's village is situated in a
lovely bay to the north-east of Santa Marta.

The Sierra Nevada de Santa Marta is considered to be the highest coastal mountain massif
in the world. Its maximum elevations are the peaks of Bolivar (18.942 ft.) and Colón
(18.892 ft.). It is today inhabited by Arhuaco, Kogi and Ijka Indians,
descendents of the Tayrona culture.

Belo, Gairaca Bay, one of the seven beautiful bays which make up Tayrona National Nature
Park, located on the foothills of the Sierra.

LA GUAJIRA

Apart from the places already mentioned, the Colombian Caribbean has other interesting spots, ranging from the peninsula of La Guajira at the border with Venezuela, to the Gulf of Urabá which borders with Panama, and in addition, Colombia's islands in the Caribbean.

The territory of La Guajira consists of the peninsula of La Guajira and part of the foothills of the Sierra Nevada de Santa Marta. The peninsula comprises upper Guajira, a semi-desertic region with sparse vegetation, corresponding to the northernmost areas of the state; and lower Guajira, which covers the rest of the peninsula, less dry although the landscape is equally arid. The foothills of the Sierra Nevada de Santa Marta contrast with these areas since the region is humid and is devoted to agriculture.

Notable on the Guajira coastline are the bays of Honda, Manaure and Tucacas, and the headlands of La Vela and Falso. Economically the state depends on mining, commerce, and services, especially state services; and to a lesser degree on cattle rearing, agriculture and tourism. Coal and sea-salt are important minerals.

Riohacha, the state capital, was founded in 1535 by Nicolás de Federmán on the shores of the Caribbean. The district of Riohacha depends mainly on services, ocean fishing, agriculture, commerce and more recently on tourism, thanks to its magnificent beaches and especially the Los Flamencos Sanctuary of Flora and Fauna.

In the district of Barrancas, situated 62 miles from Riohacha stands the loading port for the immense coal reserves of El Cerrejón, the largest open-cast mine in the world, the product of which is mostly exported. The bay of Medialuna, part of the broader bay of Portete, has been accommodated for shipping coal.

In Manaure, sea-salt is treated to make it suitable for human consumption, collected exclusively by the Wayú Indian community, which holds a government concession. The salt is obtained by evaporating salt water, which is facilitated by flat land at sea level.

Page 182, Wayú Indians in La Guajira.

Page 183, flamingos.

The peninsula of La Guajira is the northernmost territory in South America. It is populated by Indians who live in family compounds and preserve their ancestral culture and customs. It is a desert region which has such beautiful and peaceful spots as Cabo de la Vela; its economy is based on the exploitation of salt in Manaure and coal in El Cerrejón, where the largest open-cast mines in the world are found.

OTHER CITIES IN THE CARIBBEAN

VALLEDUPAR

Long before the Spanish presence in what today is the state of Cesar, the Upar Valley had been populated by Indian tribes and maintained as a strategic fortress. From this valley it is easy to control access to the southern and eastern slopes of the Sierra Nevada de Santa Marta. It is also a strategic point from which to dominate the Cesar Valley. Today the town of Valledupar is at the crossroads of trade routes and regional development, which include cotton gins, dairies, and warehouses for products transported along such routes to be stored and subsequently distributed.

Valledupar is the banking, financial, commercial and communications center of the region. Its radio stations cover the entire territory and even penetrate as far as La Guajira. The culture of the state of Cesar includes a noteworthy curiosity: in spite of having a Mediterranean-like climate, the state has no seaboard, yet it is considered to form part of the Caribbean coast. Indeed, on referring to music from the coast one would have to mention *vallenato* music - the *puya* and the *merengue* - and vallenato comes from the state of Cesar. The most important festi-

val of the vallenato is held annually in Valledupar, the state capital.

The economy of the region revolves around commerce, services, agriculture and mining. It produces excellent harvests of cotton, african palm, rice, sorghum, corn, sugar-cane, yucca, soya and cacao. Over half the state is devoted to cattle ranching and dairying. Coal mining is the state's principal mineral resource with deposits in the districts of La Jagua de Ibirico, Chiriguaná, El Paso and Becerril.

SINCELEJO

On the broad savannas of the Caribbean hinterland, at the foot of the last spurs of the hill range of San Jacinto, stands the city of Sincelejo, the capital of the state of Sucre, also known as the «Pearl of the Savanna». The city was founded around 1534 on lands inhabited by the Zenú tribes.

The main economic activities of the district of Sincelejo revolve around cattle ranching, agriculture and commerce. For the quality of the cattle in these lands, Sincelejo is known as the «Zebu Capital of Colombia». There are excellent conditions for the raising of cattle which is sold at all the principal markets in the

Page 186, sombrero vueltiao.

Page 187, House in Cereté, state of Córdoba.

On this page, one of the many expressions of folklore on the Caribbean coast: groups which are usually made up of singers, who, as in the case of Francisco el Hombre, collect the legends and real-life ocurrences of the people, employing wind instruments such as the gaita, and percussion instruments such as drums, cajas and tumbadoras, maracas and guacharacas.

On the opposite page, Montería Cathedral.

country. Agriculture is less important in the district, growing mainly corn, yucca, yams and plantain. The *corralejas* (free-for-all bullfighting) of Sincelejo are famous, around which a thriving cattle industry has developed, one of the best in the Colombian Caribbean region and in the country as a whole.

Tolú and Coveñas, situated on the Gulf of Morrosquillo, are resorts whose main income is derived from tourism. They have a broad area of private cabins which have made them an obligatory destination for thousands of travellers. In addition, Tolú preserves magnificent examples of popular architecture. The Sirenato del Mar is held here in January, with fiestas, water contests, folklore music groups and papayera bands, traditional in the region. It is also a point of access to the archipelago of San Bernardo.

Inland, in the state of Sucre near Sincelejo, lies the well-known crafts center of Sampués, famous for its Festival del *Sombrero Vueltiao*, a weaving tradition originating from the pre-Hispanic Zenú Indians who wove hats with continuous stitching and elaborate designs to protect themselves from the sun while sowing corn. This two-colored hat has become the symbol of the Caribbean coast.

MONTERÍA

Montería, the capital of the state of Córdoba, was founded in 1774 by Juan de Torrezar Díaz Pimienta with the name of San Jerónimo de Buenavista. However, since the terrain tended to become flooded it was moved by Antonio Latorre y Miranda to the spot on which it stands today, and was named San Jerónimo de Montería.

The town, at 70 ft. above sea-level, is situated on the east bank of the Sinú River, on a plain of clay soils. Its economy mainly revolves around cattle-rearing, which has transformed the town into one of the great cattle centers of the country.

Notable crops include corn, rice, cotton, yucca and plantain. Montería is a river port, the terminal on the Sinú River for the small craft which link the city with Cartagena and Barranquilla and which carry passengers and agricultural products between these ports. The western trunk road which crosses the state passes through Montería, and the majority of the cattle which leaves Córdoba for the state of Antioquia and the center of the country is transported along this road.

Main square of Valledupar, capital of the state of Cesar (above), where every year the Festival of the Legend of the Vallenato takes place and detail of the facade of a house in Ciénaga, state of Magdalena.

Below, sunsets of the Caribbean and rustic homes of the Caribbean coast, spacious and cool, employ the materials of the region and their lively colors stand out in the heat of the tropics.

Every day life of the cities and small towns of the colombian Caribbean recreates García Márquez's colorful and ever magic Macondo.

Top: Main square of Ciénaga, in the state of Magdalena.

Bottom: Very little boy in a very small boat.

SAN ANDRÉS AND OLD PROVIDENCE

The archipelago of San Andrés, Old Providence and Santa Catalina in the Caribbean deserves a special mention for its range of commercial and tourist attractions.

San Andrés, the largest of the three islands, lies 430 miles from Cartagena. Its history is different from the rest of the country, since it was originally settled in the 17th century by English Puritans and Jamaican wood-cutters who settled here with their slaves. This explains why the inhabitants of the islands preserve unique cultural traditions: the majority speak Spanish, English and a patois native dialect, and profess the Protestant faith.

The past of the archipelago is impregnated with conflict and battles. The Spanish soon began to contest the islands with their English enemies. For being near the routes of the Spanish galleons loaded down with gold and silver, the islands were the ideal base from which to attack. Pirates, corsairs, and freebooters live on in the legends of San Andrés and Old Providence. In 1793 England recognized Spanish sovereignty over the archipelago and in 1822, with the mainland territories independent from Spain, the islands adhered to what at the time was Gran Colombia. Since then the archipelago has been Colombian.

San Andrés was declared a freeport in 1953, which encouraged immigration from the Colombian mainland and exhalted commerce as one of the island's attractions, in addition to its «sea of seven colors», its beaches, its people and its famous Green Moon Festival, which brings together music from the region. Old Providence, on the other hand, continues to be a wonderfully peaceful backwater in the middle of the Caribbean.

A twenty-minute flight from San Andrés takes you to Old Providence and the neighboring island of Santa Catalina. Old Providence is of volcanic origin and has greater elevations than San Andrés. Its inhabitants have sought to preserve their autochthonous habitat and for that reason the island is the ideal place to relax. There are no large hotels, nor discoteques or commerce: nature and peacefulness hold absolute dominion over this paradise island.

The economic activities of the island revolve around agriculture, cattle ranching and fishing, which in addition to producing for local consumption also supplies a growing demand from San Andrés. Ecological tourism is another source of income.

As can be appreciated from this brief trip around the Caribbean region, the cultural mosaic generated by each state's particular characteristics bears witness to a predominantly collective spirit, expansive and euphoric, that embodies some of the clearest traits of the nation's personality. Thus it is not surprising that its music is one of the most listened to, and that its literature has become one of the most thriving and renovating in the country.

Beach on Sardine Bay, San Andrés Island.

On the islands of San Andrés and Old Providence three cultures have merged: the English,
the Spanish and that of the Afro-Antilles. The heritage of the local inhabitants is manifest in
their tongue, their music, in their traditions and beliefs, and in their architecture, which
basically employs wood and strong colors.

The sky and the sea, the people and the music, the colors and the shapes of the afrocaribbean culture are present in every corner of San Andrés and Old Providence islands.

San Andrés Island, the largest of the archipelago of San Andrés and Old Providence, is
eminently touristic; apart from its marvellous beaches and its shopping attractions it
provides all the facilities and activities which make the visitor's stay in this paradise island,
surrounded by the famous sea of seven colors, so pleasant. On this page,
boat on the beach of San Luis and the aquarium.

Old Providence is a twenty-minute trip by air from San Andrés; its inhabitants have managed to preserve the purity of their traditions and protect their natural environment.

On this page, the floating bridge which links Old Providence to Santa Catalina.

Folkloric dance in Old Town. Crab Key, one of the most visited spots on the island. The peaceful landscape of Manzanillo Bay.

ANTIOQUIA AND THE COFFEE BELT

*O*ne of the most characteristic regions of Colombia is Antioquia, inhabited by *paisas*, who have irradiated their cultural influence throughout the country, and especially in the coffee belt. This region is situated in the Andean region that forms the slopes of the Western and Central cordilleras which meet in the valley of the Cauca River. The paisa culture stretches from the state of Antioquia, covers the states of Caldas, Risaralda and Quindío, influences Tolima, and reaches as far as Cartago and Sevilla, in the north of the Valle del Cauca. To the north and west it reaches Urabá, the Pacific and Atlantic coasts, and the archipelago of San Andrés.

«An enterprising, migratory and trading people, which results in their being considered Jewish», says Luis López de Mesa (he himself being from Antioquia) in his study on the development of the Colombian people (1934). These characteristics can be seen in

Coffee farm in the state of Quindío.

The people from Antioquia truly love nature and their homes are always surrounded by flowering plants and trees. On this page, typical entrance to a coffee farm.

On the following page, two of the protagonists of colonization and its thriving economy: the mule and the jeep, which in spite of developments in transport, are still considered by the people of Antioquia to be their basic work tools.

the epic colonization process which led the people of Antioquia to populate a broad part the «national territories», which until the middle of the past century were practically uninhabited. In the course of a few decades so many new settlements and coffee plantations appeared in the region of Caldas that it changed the natural landscape of the region to become what today is known as the coffee belt. The area covered by Antioquia consists mainly of the northern part of the Central and Western cordilleras, and the valleys of the Atrato, Cauca and Magdalena rivers. During the colonial period, the economy of the region was based mainly on gold mining and the cultivation of cotton and cacao. During the 19th century the colonization movement reached its height, populating the territories of Old Caldas, and creating the basis for the coffee economy which opened up stable international markets for Colombia. During this century, all kinds of economic activities have turned Antioquia into one of the most dynamic and developed sectors of the country. The economy of the state is based on industry and commerce, but agriculture and cattle ranching is also important. Antio-quia is today the premier producer of gold and silver in the country.

With a tradition of muleteers who trans-

ported local goods over rugged territory with their mule trains, to return loaded with the product of their exchange, Antioquia has earned by sheer hard work the prominent place it enjoys in the nation, creating, thanks to such determination, a vast network of roads and villages, veritable centers of production which sustain a proud people, also known for their warmth and friendliness. The population is one of the most characteristic in the country, identifiable for its customs, food, and even its manner of speaking.

Several decades ago a radical change occurred with respect to coffee production in the region: the coffee plants, which grew beneath the shade of fruit or banana trees were replaced by unshaded plants and one-crop farming coffee varieties which were apparently more profitable, but incapable of protecting water sources, wildlife, the soil, the equilibrium of the ecosystems, and finally the rural economy which had made possible so much prosperity in the region. From then on, the region has tried different policies to diversify crops, industrialize processes, and more recently develop agrotourism, in which coffee farms house the visitor and teach him about traditional farming. Today over 200 farms form part of this project in the region, and many more plan to join the industry in the immediate future.

MEDELLÍN

Located in the Aburrá Valley in the foothills of the Central Cordillera, the capital of the state of Antioquia, Medellín, has since its founding in 1616 by Francisco Herrera Campuzano, been a dynamic nucleus in the life of the nation. The city spreads from south to north, with the Medellín River as its axis, standing at 1.550 ft. above sea-level and with a mean temperature of 73oF, which has earned it the epithet of «City of Eternal Spring». It is mainly composed of mountainous terrain, including four picturesque hills known by the names of Nutibara, El Volador, Picacho and Pan de Azúcar, with high points above 10.000ft. The only river which bathes the area is the Medellín or Porce River, and various streams which end up, together with the Medellín river, swelling the waters of the Nechí River. The «Mountain Capital» as the city is also known, is famous for its gardens, its flowers and a large variety of orchids. Eight districts make up the metropolitan area of Medellín, with a total of three and a half million inhabitants.

When the Spanish Conquistadors reached the valley of Aburrá, they found it inhabited by Tahamí and Nutabí Indians. Jerónimo Luis Tejelo, an official of the troop commanded by Jorge Robledo, reported the discovery on the 24th of August, 1541. In 1545, the governor of the Province of Antioquia, Gaspar de Rodas, descended into the valley of Aburrá where he subjugated the cacique Niquío. On the 2nd of March, 1616, the town of Medellín was founded, with the name of San Lorenzo de Aburrá, in the square of El Poblado. The founder was Francisco de Herrera y Campuzano, a judge of the Real Audiencia del Nuevo Reino de Granada and visitor general of the Province of Antioquia. The moving of the provincial capital from Santa Fe de Antioquia to Medellín was due to the latter's

great development; Francisco de Paula Santander founded it on the 17th of April, 1826.

The predominance of Medellín increased as coffee production became more important and permitted the country to enter the world economy. The industrialization of the district commenced towards the end of the past century and continues today with the development of textiles, clothing, foodstuffs, tobacco, agricultural machinery, steel, chemicals, cement and furniture, among others, which turned the city into the second industrial zone of the country and home to the leading textile industry in South America. It also has excellent public services and the most efficient generation of electricity in the country.

The city of Medellín is without doubt the most important focus of influence in the northwest of the country, and its culture influences neighboring states, the south of the state of Córdoba, the coffee belt states, and neighboring Chocó, to which important economic and social plans are directed.

The center of Medellín preserves good examples of republican architecture such as the Nutibara Hotel and the Municipal Palace; but Medellín is above all a modern city in which buildings such as those in the neighborhood of El Poblado are noteworthy for their great beauty and harmonious integration with the landscape. Coltejer Tower, with its needle-like profile, is a symbol of the city, as is the district's public services corporate building. Medellín is an orderly city, clean and dynamic, and the only city in Colombia with true mass transit: an elevated metro, inaugurated in 1995, which has integrated the city with its surrounding areas.

Medellín also enjoys intense cultural activity thanks to a group of universities, museums, theaters, libraries and first-rate artists. Such institutions include the Modern Art Museum, with a rich collection of contemporary works; the Zea Museum which has a valuable historical archive, and collections which include that donated by painter and sculptor Fernando

Page 204, panoramic view of Medellín, situated in the middle of the Aburrá Valley. Thanks to its pleasant climate, it has been called «the city of eternal spring».

During the month of August the flower-bearers parade takes place. Flower growers who make beautfiful and original arrangements load them onto their shoulders and show them off on the streets of Medellín. This is the most authentic festival of the city.

Botero, originally from Medellín; the Anthropological Museum, housing a comprehensive collection of pre-Columbian objects; the House and Museum of Pedro Nel Gómez, devoted to his prolific and important work; and the Historical Archive of Antioquia, whose extensive collection of documents bear witness to the rich history of both the city and the region since colonial times.

A notable fact about Medellín is the proliferation of three-dimensional works, generally of high quality, which populate the streets and parks of the city, and also in many facades and entrances. The famous «Fat Wo-man» by Botero in the city center is a traditional meeting point.

Notable events include La Candelaria Bullfighting Fair, which takes place every year in February; the Festival de la Trova which presents the region's most typical popular musical expressions, in August; the Colombiatex Show, which presents the season's textiles and fashion,

the autochthonous Feria de la Antioqueñidad, the National Horse Show, and the Book Fair, which has been taking place for a number of years and is always full of surprises.

The Flower Show takes place between the 1st and 7th of August in Medellín, a traditional exhibition whose central event is the parade of the silleteros: hundreds of rural flower-growers come down the mountains wearing typical costumes and carrying chairs on their shoulders bedecked with splendid floral arrangements, to music performed by guitar players and typical bands, alongside dance groups which accompany the flower-bearers.

Santa Fe de Antioquia lies 47 miles from Medellín on the Carretera al Mar. It was the first capital of the province, founded by Mariscal Jorge Robledo in 1541. It is one of the most beautiful and best-preserved colonial villages in the country, with notable buildings such as its Cathedral, built between 1799 and 1837.

The first Librería Nacional in Colombia was founded 57 years ago in the city of Barranquilla, by Don Jesús María Ordóñez, born in Santander who spent his adolescence and youth in the city of La Habana where he trained as a bookseller working in the most important book store in America at the time, La Cultural de La Habana. On returning to Colombia, Ordóñez arrived in the city of Barranquilla which in the 1940s was called the Golden Gate of Colombia, for its commercial, industrial and cultural importance. Since he was a great bookseller and a man of broad commercial vision, he completely change the concept which until that moment he had about the sale of books, and this new bookstore was not just one more in the city.

With the book stores consolidated and the success of the new concept in the sale of books through self-service demonstrated, new book stores were opened in other cities of the country. In 1996 the first Librería Nacional was opened in Medellín in the San Diego shopping mall. The quality of the publications and the success obtained in this city has led the managers of the company to consider creating new branches in the capital of Antioquia.

The *Compañía Nacional de Chocolates* is a symbol of the Colombian productive sector.

It was founded in Medellín in 1920, when a visionary group of businessmen from Antioquia saw a promising future in the industrialization of cacao.

From its beginnings until the dawn of the twenty-first century, the Company has consolidated its operations and has earned a nationally-recognized leadership for the broad range of its portfolio, with high quality products which cover the different traditional consumer lines and those which reflect new lifestyles, to respond to the needs of consumers. It has broadened into international markets with important undertakings, mainly through the export of coffee and the attainment of strategic alliances which, together with the clear goal of opening up new markets, permit it to compete today in the global·economy.

Its subsidiaries, Industria Colombiana de Café - Colcafé, Fábrica de Café La Bastilla, Industria Colombiana de Chocolates La Especial and its investments in other important food companies, make up the industrial complex of this dynamic sector in Colombia and in the regional markets of South America, where it holds an outstanding position.

Colombia»s second city, Medellín, with a population of almost three and a half million inhabitants, has the most modern infrastructure in the country thanks to the vitality of its people, and an extensive metropolitan area which covers eight districts.

Previous page, panoramic view of the city center and on this page, the metro which, inaugurated in December 1995, crosses the Aburrá Valley from one end to the other.

In spite of significant transformations in the city»s urban stracutre, many buildings of considerable architectural value have been preserved, such as the Metropolitan Basilica situated on the Plaza de Bolivar, the church of San Ignacio and the University of Antioquia, whose magnificent remodelling was completed recently, and the republican-style railway station. Beautiful sculptures have also been erected in the city, such as those created by Fernando Botero, one of the city most illustrious sons.

Scientific research, high technology and quality service make the Santa María Cardiovascular Clinic the specialists center of your heart.

Created 32 years ago by the Mariana Congregation - Santa María Foundation, devoted to the prevention, diagnosis, treatment and rehabilitation of patients with cardiovascular problems, placed Colombia in 1985 in the world-class scientific arena, thanks to the first heart transplant undertaken and recently the first lung transplant.

One of the city»s main attractions is its vibrant business activity, whose development can be appreciated in the large shopping malls, such as Villanueva which is housed in the former cloister of the Seminary.

Antioquia was a pioneer in the creation and development of the textile industry which, together with apparel, are important sources of work and income.

The Coltejer building is a symbol of modern Medellín.

BECAUSE YOU DESERVE THE BEST, Sheraton International invites you to enjoy the comforts of a modern first-class hotel, winner of two Chairman'_ Club awards for the most improved service and highest guest satisfaction ratings. Located beside the up-scale Oviedo Shopping Mall, Four Points Sheraton offers 123 rooms, ample meeting rooms for up to 300 guests, a business center, sauna and steam rooms, and an excercise area and pool. The «Magallanes» restaurant will tempt you with a broad range of gastronomical delights, while «La Tertulia» lobby bar provides the perfect ambience to toast with your friends.

Four Points Medellin Sheraton Hotel

Antioquia State Railroad Station, a recently restored building. Its republican style makes contrast with the modern architecture that has evolved in its surroundings.

It is a leading Colombian company in the VERTICAL TRANSPORT sector, with over 20 years of experience in the manufacture, assembly and maintenance of elevators, mechanical stairs and ramps, forklift trucks and car transporters. At present it has branches in eight cities in Colombia and exports to Tailand, Arabia, China, Kuwait, Venezuela and Central America. It is also the representative of Allen Bradley for Colombia, Alimak Elevator Co., Unistrut, Hadco and Montgomery KONE. It is a General Electric OEM and the manufacturer of IMELEC electrical boards.

The La Alpujarra Administrative Center is Medellín»s most modern administrative complex. The municipal and state governments are located here, and around it important urban renewal projects have been developed.

The Administrative Center»s public space is decorated, as occurs in the majority of the city, with beautiful monuments.

Medellin citizens and authorities for long time now have assumed the task of building public
space as the scenario for a pleasent coexistence. As a consequence of that, almost every
building, mall and path has been carefully planned and constucted in order to become a way
to improve everybody's life quality.

What is important for you is important for us, too. Because we know what you want, we will make of your visit to our hotel a very pleasant experience.

Let us get to know you better through each of your visits. Enjoy those little details that make you feel at home: our excellent service and the best location in town.

Our extraordinary facilities guarantee you the most comfortable stay. 85 ample rooms, banquet and convention rooms, restaurant, coffee shop, pool, gymnasium, and a high technology communication and computer system.

*Carrera 43A 4 sur-75 Avenida El Poblado • Tel.: 268 5555 - Fax: 268 6949
E-mail: 104551.341@COMPUSERVE.COM
Medellin - Colombia*

Modern architectural currents achieve their maximum expression in the metropolitan area of Medellin. The headquarters of public institutions in the city center and the José María Córdova airport near the village of Rionegro are good examples of Medellin»s development, the nation»s second-largest city and number one in urban development.

The geographic location of Medellin in the heart of the Aburrá Valley with its privileged climate, make the region one of the richest in flower production.

From August 1 thru 7 the city celebrates the Flower Fair, a traditional fiesta whose central event is the parade of flower-bearers which brings together farmers who come down the mountains loaded with splendid floral arrangements. The parade is accompanied by dance groups, stringed instrument players and typical bands.

CLÍNICA LAS AMÉRICAS

Clínica Las Américas is committed to being the best option in the city of Medellín when it comes to high technology health services with humane, medical and scientific quality. Currently it offers more than fifty medical specialities, seven hospitalization stories with 156 beds, and fifteen operating rooms. Some of the most outstanding services and units of this medical institution are the Intensive Care Unit, the Oncology Institute, a medical laboratory, the Emergency Room, cardiology, cardiovascular surgery, general and specialized surgery, gynaecology, obstetrics and newborn care, diagnostic images, dialysis, pathology, nuclear medicine, and physical therapy and rehabilitation.

SUSALUD is a subsidiary of SURAMERICANA, devoted to improving the quality of life of the Colombian people, through health plans and medical and dental services in its subsidiary companies in the country's main cities. Its capacity, vision and dynamism make it a leading company in the health sector in Colombia.

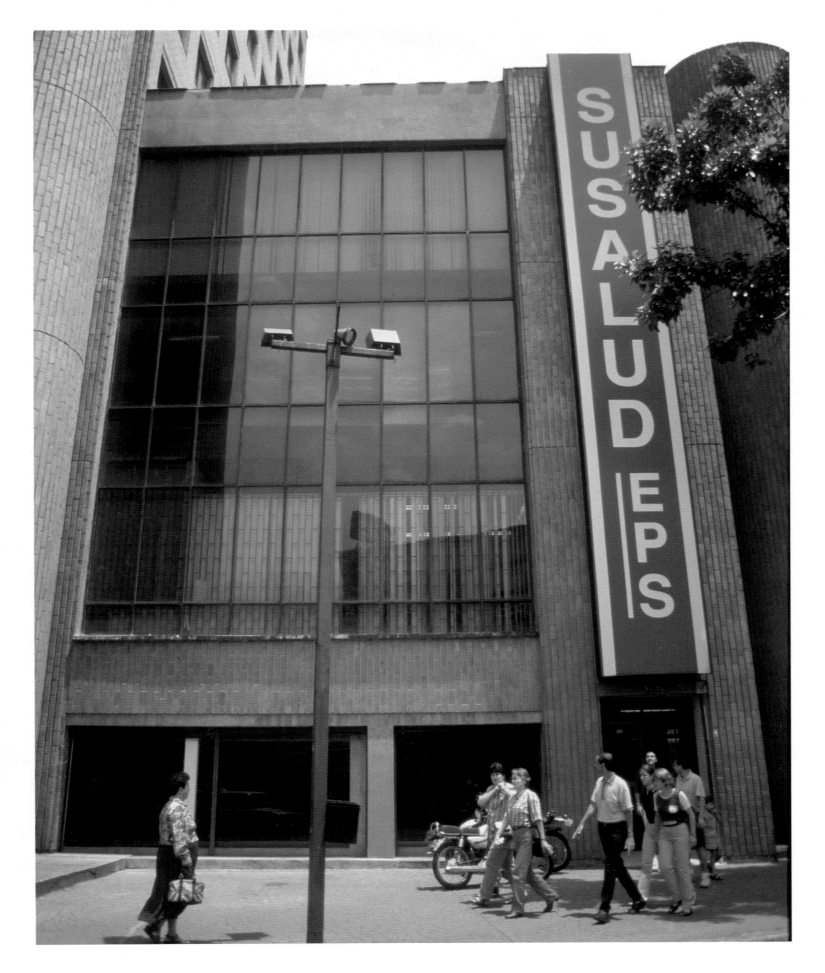

Industrias HACEB is a company from Antioquia which began in 1940 with the basic idea of repairing electrical appliances. It later manufactured grills with which the trademark gained national prestige. It then diversified with a broad range of high quality electrical and gas appliances: grills with two and three plates, stoves or kitchenettes, ovens, water heaters and both conventional and no frost refrigerators. In 1997 it received the ISO 9001 Quality Assurance Certificate for its refrigeration production line. It has a team of over 1.800 employees who work at its Autopista Sur and Copacabana plants. At present it is building a modern production plant in Copacabana.

The majority of the villages near Medellin preserve the traditional architecture of colonization by Antioquia, and also the typical means of transport such as the bus de escalera which replaced the mule of the former muleteers. Santafé de Antioquia (upper right), one of the most beautiful towns in the region, was the first capital the state had. In Jardín (lower left), to the south of the capital of Antioquia, the traditions of the past century are preserved almost intact. One of the country»s most surprising engineering works is the Orient suspension bridge, which was declared a national monument.

THE COFFEE BELT

Towards 1870 the so-called «national territories», which constituted three quarters of the country, were practically uninhabited. 42% of the population of Colombia was concentrated in the Eastern Cordillera, while the wide, fertile plains were not made use of. The broadening of the agricultural frontier became a priority because of social pressures resulting from successive civil wars which tore the country apart during the past century. From the extreme north of the Central Cordillera a movement began called the «colonization of Antioquia», which was perhaps the most important social and economic phenomenon of the 19th century after Independence, since it signified the demographic recovery of the country, populating the slopes of the Central and Western cordilleras. The founding of Salamina and Aguadas was a milestone in this migratory process, which greatly broadened the economic, social and political frontier of Antioquia. It also resulted in towns such as Pácora, Quinchía, Neira, Manizales, Fresno, Chinchiná, Líbano, Apía, Samaná, Filandia, Armenia and Monte-negro being established. The initiative continued up until the beginning of the 20th century, creating new settlements in

the territories of Tolima and Valle del Cauca, and covering what is known as Great Caldas. Parallel events which contributed to make the colonizing movement more significant were the opening of railway lines which linked the countryside with the ports on the Magdalena and Cauca rivers, and the expansion of coffee-growing with which Colombia fully entered international markets. The result of such trade was the colossal formation of capital, which made possible the emergence of other industries and a financial sector in Antioquia. This permitted the state to diversify its economy, an expansion which did not occur in other regions. The Coffee Belt, which developed in Old Caldas, dedicated practically all its land to the cultivation of coffee, creating a common culture in the region. This characteristic is notable in the food, the family and the «architecture of colonization», in which the use of bamboo and other woods predominate, together with a decoration in vivid colors, and broad corridors brimming with flowers which encircle the houses.

Three different states emerged from Old Caldas, grouped around thriving towns which rivaled each other in the region. Caldas with Manizales

as its capital, Quindío with Armenia as its capital and Risaralda with Pereira as its capital, constitute the «coffee axis» which for several decades formed the backbone of the principal export product of the country. Indeed, it can be said that the region has been the economic heart of the country for a good part of this century, since in addition to being at the physical center of the Colombia, it supplied the necessary foreign exchange for the development of the nation, and in addition is connected with the rest of the country by an excellent road network.

NATURE PARKS

The entire coffee region spreads out over the Central Cordillera, the highest of the three cordilleras which cross Colombia. Los Nevados National Nature Park, created in 1974, is situated in this mountainous massif and crosses part the states of Caldas, Risaralda, Quindío and Tolima. It covers an area of 220 sq. miles, with high points which range from 8.000 to 18.000 ft. above sea-level, and has a variety of climates which include those corresponding to high Andean forest, páramo, and perpetual snow.

A large quantity of rivers and streams originate in this massif, which provide water to the entire central region of Colombia. Here the visitor can admire the majesty of the snow-capped peaks of the the Nevado del Ruiz Volcano, an imposing mountain 17.710 ft. high and one of the highest in Colombia; the Nevado del Cisne, at 15.740 ft.; the Nevado de Santa Isabel at 16.230 ft., the most beautiful of the group with its summit of three peaks; the Nevado del Quindío at 15.740 ft., and the Nevado del Tolima at 17.100 ft.. They represent a real challenge for mountaineers, since access to these peaks is difficult.

CALDAS

The majority of the state of Caldas is situated in a warm or sub-Andean climate in the Central Cordillera, with very suitable soils for the cultivation of coffee - for which reason the state is one of the leading coffee producers in the country. Other crops are cultivated such as sugar cane, yucca, corn, beans and potatoes. In 1905, with the new territorial division of the country, the state of Caldas was created, with Manizales as its capital. In 1966 the states of Risaralda and Quindío seceded from its territory, and together

The coffee belt is situated in a mountainous region whose highest points are covered by perpetual snow. Its land, enriched by former volcanic eruptions, are the most suitable for the intensive farming of the best mild coffee in the world. The villages in the region have had to adapt their architecture to the difficult terrain. Page 228, the snow peak of the Ruiz Volcano.

Page 229, panoramic view of Aguadas, state of Caldas.

they are known as «Old Caldas». Today the state of Caldas consists of 25 districts.

The state capital, Manizales was founded in 1849, and is the oldest of the three coffee capitals. It is situated in very rugged terrain at 7.000 ft. above sea-level, which gives it a peculiar urban form of very steep streets. The Nevado del Ruiz Volcano rises nearby at 17.710 ft. above sea-level. Today Manizales is a modern city which grows at a fast pace. Although its economy continues to revolve around coffee, there are also diverse industries, an important commerce, and financial services.

Throughout its history, Manizales has been characterized as one of the most traditional cultural and educational centers in Colombia, with such important institutions as the Fine Arts Palace, universities of national standing, technical centers of higher education and numerous schools.

Every September since 1969, the International Theater Festival has taken place in Manizales, in which professional, university, experimental, street and pantomime groups of the country and from abroad participate. The Manizales Fair, which

takes place between the 2nd and 6th of January each year, has become one of the most important popular festivals in the country.

Every two years, in the neighboring town of Riosucio, one of the most singular festivals takes place: the Devil's Carnival, at which a benign devil is worshipped amidst processions which allude, with irony and humor, to national and international events.

RISARALDA

The state of Risaralda is a mountainous region in the Central and Western cordilleras and a flat region in the Risaralda River Valley. Its lands are very fertile, consisting of volcanic ash, and its agriculture is mainly coffee-growing and sugar cane. Mining and cattle ranching is representative of different parts of the state, and there has been en extraordinary growth in industry in recent years, especially in the district of Dosquebradas and in Pereira, its capital, which has become the main pole of development of the region. The state was created in 1966 and consists of 14 districts.

Pereira, the capital of Risaralda, was founded in 1863 on the

banks of the Otún River by settlers of Antioquia and Valle del Cauca, led by the priest Remigio Antonio Cañarte. In a short time, and thanks to the drive of its people, Pereira has become the fifth pole of industrial development of the country, in which clothing and metal manufacture predominate. Pereira is known by its epithets «City without Doors» and «The Pearl of the Otún», and has an important Convention Center and first-rate hotels.

The sculptor Rodrigo Arenas Betancourt built a dynamic monument, known as the Unclothed Bolívar, for Pereira's central square, while his Chained Prometheus stands in the Technological University. The Monument to the Founders is another of his works, in which the «fire - man» is notable, a homage to the efforts and courage of the region's predecessors; also the Christ without a Cross in the Sanctuary of Our Lady of Fatima.

7 miles from Pereira, on the road to Manizales, stands Santa Rosa de Cabal, founded in 1844, of notable rural architecture.

QUINDÍO

The state of Quindío spreads out over the western slopes of the Central Cordillera. The area is a fertile hydrographic depression, for the most part of rugged terrain although some areas possess a gentle relief. It has a great variety of climates, although a warm climate predominates. In addition to coffee, which covers most of the state, plantain, yucca, sugar cane, cacao, avocado and numerous tropical fruits such as maracuyá, pithaya, passion-fruit and watermelon are grown. Cattle ranching, commerce and a manufacturing industry are also notable activities.

In 1966, with the division of Caldas, Quindío became an independent state comprising 12 districts.

Armenia, the state capital, was founded in 1889 by a group of settlers led by Jesús María Ocampo, but its first inhabitants date from 1870. In spite of being the youngest of the state capitals of the «coffee axis», human intervention on the landscape is notable: apart from agriculture, in which coffee dominates, it is evidenced in the traditional rural architecture of the colonization, the management of the river basins and streams, and reforestation, which has returned to the area what had been removed by the axe - which, in fact, is the region's symbol. Apart from coffee, the area produces corn, beans, yucca, plantain and fruit. The districts which make up Quindío are near to

*The typical architecture of Antioquia, present in every village in the coffee belt, is epitomize
by the harmonious and brilliant use of color on doors and windows.*

Page 230, exterior of a house in Montenegro, Quindío.

each other and have maintained a constant development, which gives the state one of the highest and homogeneous levels in the quality of life.

Armenia is dubbed the «Miracle City» for the drive of its friendly and enterprising people. Its parks, famous for their excellent design and lush vegetation, are the pride of the inhabitants.

Close to Armenia lies the Coffee Park, which has an excellent display of the different species of coffee plant, a fine example of a typical coffee farm, and the different tasks which make up the coffee culture that gives the region its flavor and aroma.

Quindío is a state through which you can easily travel, on good roads, and appreciate incomparable landscapes, coffee haciendas (many of which offer lodging), and lovely villages which bear witness to the architecture of colonization in Antioquia. The town of Calarcá was founded in 1886 by settlers from Antioquia, being the birthplace of the poet Luis Vidales. The town's name evokes the cacique Calarcá, chief of the Pijao Indians who fiercely resisted the Spanish troops. The historical center of Calarcá was declared a national monument for its tradi-

tional bamboo and adobe architecture. Salento is considered to be the home of the National Tree, the wax palm of Quindío. Cocora Valley can be observed from Alto de la Cruz, situated 7 miles from the town, where hundreds of such palms proudly stand erect. Other towns include Montenegro, founded in 1892, where the Park and Museum of the Coffee Culture is located, dedicated to illustrate everything related to coffee from the sowing of the bean to the final product; Córdoba, to the south of the state, known for the famous Bamboo-Guadua Experimental Center, where multiple uses for this plant are researched; Pijao, winner of «The prettiest village in Quindío» contest; and Génova, surrounded by high mountains, ideal for mountaineering and ecotourism.

Antioquia and the coffee belt make up a landscape which is essential to the comprehension of one of the most outstanding facets of its people, who with faith, hard work and a spirit of adventure have imposed the personality of the paisa culture on their environment, and where the positive attributes of the Colombian character can be more easily recognized.

One of the coffee region»s main attractions is Los Nevados National Nature Park, whose principal heights are the snow peaks of the Ruiz, El Cisne, Santa Isabel, Quindío and Tolima volcanoes. The majestic Otún Lake lies admidst them (page 232).

On this page, Riosucio, in the state of Caldas, is famous for its Festival del Diablo, a traditional celebration which takes place every two years during the first few days of January; and the village of Pácora, famous for the hospitality of its people.

Manizales, typified by elegance and class, is situated at the crossroads between the states of Antioquia, Cauca, Cundinamarca and Tolima and grew as a result of trade, becoming a vital regional center and the capital of the state of Caldas. In the 1920s, the town was destroyed by several fires, which is why its architecture has a strong European influence. Manizales Fair, which takes place in the first week of January, is famous for bull fighting and for the International Coffee Beauty Contest. On the following page, the cathedral, one of the symbols of the city.

Pereira, the «Pearl of the Otún River», is the city which has had the greatest industrial a rban development in the coffee belt. Its broad metropolitan area reaches as far as the di Dosquebradas and has an excellent road network, including the modern «Gésar Gavi viaduct which facilitates the traffic.

The Plaza de Bolivar is the heart of the city; here the majority of popular events take place.
The unclothed Bolivar, the symbol of the city, is considered to be one of the greatest works of
sculptor Rodrigo Arenas Betancur from Antioquia.

On one side of the plaza stands the cathedral of Nuestra Señora de la Pobreza.

Master Valencia dubbed Armenia, the capital of the state of Quindío, the «Miracle City of Colombia», for the iron will of its inhabitants, inheritors of the colonizing spirit of their forebears. On this page, two aspects of the Plaza de Bolívar: the Monument to Effort, by Rodrigo Arenas Betancur and the stained-glass windows of the cathedral of the Inmaculada Concepción, a modern structure, whose layout is in the form of a latin cross.

On this page, panoramic view of the city of Armenia and the Quimbaya Museum, winner of the National Prize for Architecture 1986 and the work of architect Rogelio Salmona. It houses a valuable collection of gold and pottery work by the pre-Columbian Quimbaya Indian culture, which made wonderful objects recognized internationally for their perfection and the beauty of their designs.

The topography of the states which make up the coffee belt, characteristic of the mountain slopes of the Central and Western cordilleras, is precipitous and possesses very rich soils which produce a large quantitiy of native species, notably an immense variety of orchids and wax palm, the species of palm which grows at a higher elevation (up to 11.500 ft. above sea level) and which is considered the national tree.

Amidst the natural beauty of this area, coffee plantations spread out under the shade of banana and fruit trees.

The inhabitants of the coffee region have proudly preserved their customs and way of looking at life. One of the most autochthonous expressions is the vivid color which they give to the outside of their houses, both rural and urban, to the local buses and to all the manifestations of the regional ambience.

On this page: a bus escalera, a farm in Montenegro, state of Quindío, Quimbaya Park, and a monument in the National Coffee Park.

THE PACIFIC REGION

The region of the Colombian Pacific coast does not do justice to its name, since it is considered to be one of the wildest areas in the country. Some spots have an annual rainfall of 10.000 mm and equally high humidity, which becomes concentrated by the thickness of the jungle, and makes human survival difficult in most of the region.

When Vasco Núñez de Balboa named it the «Other Sea» in 1513, the discovery of the Pacific was evidence that America was a different continent from the Asia which Columbus thought he had found by sailing to the west. The Colombian Pacific coast covers 800 miles of seaboard from the Darien region on the border with Panama, in the north-west, down to the border with Ecuador in the south. This area, a narrow strip of territory between the Pacific Ocean and the Western

Page 242, Tebaida Bay on the Pacific coast.

Cordillera, with an abundance of precious metals and natural resources, is one of the most beautiful and exotic places in Colombia, and has one of the richest ecosystems and biodiversity on the planet. According to botanist Alwin Gentry, the Colombian Pacific jungle is the most profuse in vegetable species in the world. In some parts of the study, this scientist has found up to 265 different species of plants per hectare - the majority endemic in the region, which means that they are not found anywhere else on Earth.

Four states have coasts on the Pacific: Chocó, Valle del Cauca, Cauca and Nariño. The main towns of the region are Quibdó, capital of Chocó, on the banks of the Atrato River; Buenaventura, in the state of Valle, the main port on the Colombian Pacific coast and one of the most important in South America on the Pacific side; the port of Tumaco, situated in the state of Nariño, is the second port on this ocean. The seaboard of the state of Cauca runs between Buenaventura and Tumaco, one of the least densely populated regions in the country.

The economy of the Pacific region depends to a large extent on forestry, fishing, and especially on gold and platinum mining. The west coast of Colombia looks expectantly towards the

Pacific Basin, one of the most thriving regions in the world, with a view to develop its enormous potential for trade.

The Tumaco culture evolved between 500 BC and 1000 AD; they practised alluvial mining, that is to say, panning for gold in river beds or streams, just as it continues to be practised in the region today. Indeed, the oldest known gold artefacts belong to this culture: some thin gold wires of great purity, hammered employing a complex technique, with which they manufactured diadems, nose rings, necklaces, pectoral ornaments, masks and anthropomorphic figures with elongated heads. Pottery was also developed by the Tumaco culture and their objects are highly esteemed. This society grew corn, fished, and built their houses on stilts throughout the islands formed by the deltas of the numerous rivers and streams which flow into the Pacific Ocean.

In pre-Hispanic times the Cuna Indians had also settled in the region, in the Gulf of Urabá and lower Atrato River, the Chocoes or Citarás in the upper Atrato, the Noanamás and Emberás in the depression of the San Juan River, and the Baudoes on the Pacific coast. Today nearly a million people live together in the «bio-geographic province of Chocó», the majority of Afro-Colombian origin, mestizos and Indian communities

The Pacific coast is one of the wettest on Earth, with an annual rainfall of over 10.000 mm in the Atrato river basin. At some spots, the virgin jungle reaches down to the sea. Page 244, Cape Marzo.

The Pacific region is one of the richest in biodiversity in the world and its natural resources have been preserved as a result of the inhospitable environment. On this page, alligator near the Baudó River.

such as the Cuna, Emberá-Katío, Waunana and Kwaiker tribes, distributed in almost sixty reserves.

During the Colony, one of the pillars of the regional economy was mining, the great majority of whose product was sent to Spain. The great demand for gold encouraged the search for mines, which was rewarded with the discovery of rich deposits in the north-west of the country, the explotation of which depended on Indian labor. The arduous conditions of the jungle were too much for the strength of many natives, which necessitated introducing negro labor under slavery. From then on the black population has become the predominant race in the region. At present 85% of the population on the Pacific coast are thought to be descendents of Africans.

CHOCÓ

The state of Chocó consists mainly of a broad plain, bordered to the east by the Western Cordillera and to the west by the Baudó Hills through which the Atrato River passes, considered to be one of the biggest rivers in the world in relation to its length, and which flows

out into the Caribbean; and the San Juan River, shorter in length, which flows into the Pacific Ocean. In the Atrato valley there is a dense jungle, floodable and swampy, known as the Darien Gap. The San Juan valley is considered to be one of world's richest areas in platinum.

A large part of Chocó is located in the area of Equatorial calm, which is the cause of intense rainfall, continuing throughout the year, with very few dry days and an annual rainfall of over 10.000 cubic millimeters. As a result, the vegetation which covers the state is one of the most varied in the world. However, the soils have little potential for farming.

Comprising 21 districts, the economy of the state is mainly dependent on mining, especially gold, platinum and silver, and on lumbering in both homogeneous and heterogeneous forests such as mangrove, guandal, natal and catival, among others, principally for export, with facilities for both river and sea transport.

Chocó is also the only state in Colombia which has coasts on both oceans, and for this reason many projects to connect the two oceans have been developed throughout

On this page, view of the bay of Buenaventura, the main Colombian port on the Pacific. On the following page, market in Guapi, a coastal village whose inhabitants, the majority descendents of African slaves, exploit gold, wood and plantain.

the history of the region. Its name derives from the Indian community of the Chocoes, who share their territory with the predominant black communities.

Bahía Solano, also known as Ciudad Mutis, is one of the main tourist destinations on the Pacific coast, situated on the Gulf of Cupica. Its main attraction is ocean fishing, and is visited by sportsmen from all over the world. It also attractive for its humid, tropical jungle landscape where the beauty of the sea and jungle blend together. Towards the north of Bahía Solano there are several excellent spots for fishing such as Cabo Marzo. A little to the south of Bahía Solano lies Utría Sound, declared a National Park in 1987, with four different ecosystems: coral reef, mangrove, sound, and tropical forest.

On the Caribbean coast and bordering with Panama lies Acandí, which attracts considerable tourism to the beaches of Capurganá and Sapzurro on the Gulf of Urabá. The region is a big banana producer.

Quibdó is situated on the east bank of the Atrato River on a broad

and beautiful plain with high temperatures, a humid atmosphere and intense rainfall. It is the state capital.

Quibdó is the center for trade in Chocó and the most important port on the Atrato River. It maintains an active commerce with the majority of the districts of the state, with villages on the Gulf of Urabá on the Caribbean coast, and with Medellín, from where both Quibdó and the state of Chocó obtain basic goods, and foodstuffs to complement the diet of their inhabitants. As with the rest of the state, its main economic activity is mining and lumbering.

A special attraction of the Chocó is Los Katíos National Nature Park, shared by the states of Chocó and Antioquia and covering 280 sq. miles. The park is adjacent to the Darien National Park in Panama, and its objective is to study the environmental impact of building the Panamerican Highway on the region's endemic species. The special charactistics of the park earned it the title of «World Heritage» by Unesco in 1994. The main characteristics of this reserve are the variety of its soils, plains

which do not flood, swamplands and ciénagas, and rolling hills.

Utría Sound, a National Nature Park with a land and marine area of 210 sq. miles, covers the districts of Bahía Solano, Nuquí, Bojayá and Alto Baudó. Here four of the most threatened ecosystems are found: mangrove, estuaries, coral reefs and rain forest. The contrast between the rain forest and the steep mountain slopes which reach down to the sea is one of the most notable aspects of the landscape. The area is also important for the abundance of marine life, especially the seasonal presence of whales.

Buenaventura is Colombia's main port on the Pacific, three hours from Cali on a road which crosses the Western Cordillera. Founded in 1539 by Captain Juan de Ladrilleros, the port belongs today to the state of Valle del Cauca. Its importance dates back to the close of the 18th century, when the administration of the gold mines of Chocó and Barbacoas was established here, lasting until the beginning of this century.

The Farallones National Nature Park of Cali is situated on the ridge of the Western Cordillera in the state of Valle, in the districts of Cali, Jamundí, Dagua and Buenaventura. It has an area

of 580 sq. miles, covering four climatic zones, with temperatures which vary between 77oF in low-lying areas and 41oF on the peaks, the highest of which are over 14.000 ft. high. The name of the park comes from the veins of the mountains which stick out along the ridge of the Western Cordillera and which form a chain of steep crags.

As mentioned previously, the Pacific coast in the state of Cauca is one of the most sparsely inhabited in Colombia. Guapi and Timbiquí, on the rivers of the same name, are the most notable settlements. Guapi became a district in 1816 and is the most important town on the Cauca coast. The population is black and its economy is based on agriculture, fishing, basket weaving with vegetable fibers, and gold mining.

Turned into a penal colony for many years, Gorgona Island became a National Park in 1985 for its enormous biodiversity in flora and fauna and its coral reefs, which draw humpbacked whales to the area every year. The island belongs to the state of Cauca, located 35 miles from Guapi. It is equidistant from the two main ports on the Colombian Pacific: 90 miles from Buenaventura and Tumaco. It has an area of 9

The Colombian Pacific coast has basically two well-defined regions: the northern part is typified by the narrowness of its continental platform and the presence of rocky cliffs. The southern part has a broad continental platform and has the largest and most widespread mangrove swamps in the country.

sq. miles, 6 miles long and a half wide, while the reserve has an area of 188 sq. miles, including the island of Gorgonilla.

After a trip of over 2.500 miles from the Antarctic, humpbacked whales in groups of a hundred or so reach the waters around Gorgona Island in the month of July. Their behavior is unpredictable, but it is possible to see them rolling around producing large waves as they fall back into the water, showing off their beauty. In the mating season you can hear the beautiful and mysterious melodies which the males emit. The island is frequented by ecological tourism, as are the neighboring islands of Gorgonilla and Malpelo.

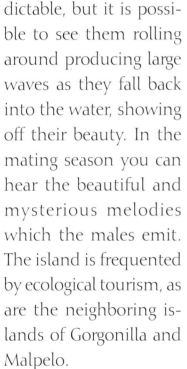

The Conservation Unit of Munchique is situated on the western slopes of the Western Cordillera in the state of Cauca, in the district of El Tambo. It covers 170 sq. miles of rugged terrain with steep slopes, and with high points which range between 1.800 and 10.700 ft. and temperatures which vary between 46 and 81oF. Munchique Park has a great variety of tree species which belong to forests

adapted to hot, warm and cold climatic zones. Its fauna is notable for the great variety of birds, with over 420 documented species, many of which are endemic to the region.

Tumaco is one of the most important settlements on the Pacific coast in the state of Nariño, for being a seaport located 190 miles from Pasto, the state capital. The settlement was founded at the end of the eighteenth century by the Tuma Indians. Today it is the second port on the Colombian Pacific, with a population of over 100.000 inhabitants.

Sanquianga National Nature Park is situated in this region, taking its name from the river and bay. The park is part of the archeological area of the pre-Hispanic Tumaco culture and covers over 300 sq. miles. Its principal characteristic is an important area of mangrove, a species in serious danger throughout the world, yet the most productive ecosystem that exists. The area is criss-crossed by an infinite number of esturaries considerably affected by the tides.

Page 250, rocky coastline and cliff in the Gulf of Cupica.

On the northern part of the Pacific coast there are both natural and cultural manifestations. Near Utría Sound, hump-backed whales can be seen which arrive every year around the month of September. On the banks of the ciénagas lining the river courses, the vegetation is especially lush. Diverse spots on the coast are inhabited by Indian groups such as the Embera Indians, who continue to preserve their ancestral customs. Puerto Mutis is a place where you can sense the humidity of the environment.

The Hotel Estación, in the port of Buenaventura, is a magnificent construction from the 1930s, which has been remodeled; today it is one of the most comfortable and beautiful places at which to stay. From its corridors you can contemplate spectaular sunsets in the bay and witness the vibrant port activity.

As a result of racial and cultural mestizaje, the Pacific coast is rich in culture, which includes varied musical rhythms of Indian, African and Europen origin , notably the contradanza, la jota and especially the currulao and the mapalé.

The local inhabitants gather at sunset to produce rythmical sounds, in which percussion instruments predominate.

The southern part of the Pacific coast belongs to the states of Cauca and Nariño; it is a jungle region where mangrove swamps abound. Some Indian tribes live there who preserve their traditions, although the predominant race is negro.

On this page: necklace of the Embera Indians, market in the port of Guapi and two aspects of Bocagrande, the main resort of the state of Nariño, very near Tumaco, the second port on the Pacific coast.

THE ANDEAN SOUTH

The south-west of the Andean region is covered by the states of Valle del Cauca, Cauca, and Nariño, which borders with Ecuador. The region is quite rugged, with its main settlements located in the Andean region, but because of its varied topography all climatic regions are present, from the high peaks of volcanoes and perpetual snows, to the tropical zones of the Pacific coast.

During colonial times, the province of Cauca was one of the most properous and influential in Nueva Granada, covering the present-day states of Valle, Cauca, Nariño, part of Old Caldas, and Caquetá. Its capital was the town of Popayán, inhabited by Nueva Granada's most powerful aristocracy, composed of landowners, miners and merchants. Popayán became what the historian of Latin American cities, José Luis Romero, called a «patriarchal society», but given the magnitude of the agricultural and mining companies which were set up, the town was obliged to import slave

Sorghum plantation in the state of Valle de Cauca.

On this page, the llama, an animal which had great importance in the world of the Incas.

The elegant way of life of the aristocrats of the town of Popayán is manifest in the architecture and ornamentation of the large houses in which they have lived since colonial times and which bear witness to their ancestral traditions. On the following page, a region of small farmers in the state of Nariño, in which the cultivation of sisal predominates. Everyday objects are made from it, such as sacks, hats and beautiful crafts.

labor, which inserted a slavery-based society into the town's social composition.

Historically the inhabitants of Cauca and Valle have closer ties with each other than they have with their neighbors in Nariño, called *pastusos*. By tradition the name *caucanos* has been given to such notable people of Colombian history as Francisco José de Caldas, Camilo Torres, Tomás Cipriano de Mosquera, José Hilario López, Sergio Arboleda, Jorge Isaacs and Guillermo Valencia, to mention only some of the notables who were born either in Cauca or in Valle del Cauca. Pastusos have more in common with Ecuador, since Sebastián de Belalcázar attached the region (whose capital is San Juan de Pasto) to the Audience of Quito in 1541. After independence from Spain, in 1819, the region became part of the province of Popayán, and in 1821 of the state of Cauca, until in 1904 the state of Nariño was born.

The cultural mosaic of the Andean South is one of the richest in Colombia and has given rise to the myth of the happy *valluno*, the serious *caucano* and the ingenuous and obliging modesty of the *pastuso*. It has also given rise to the heroic deeds of the resistance put up by escaped slaves on the Palo River and the growth of fugitive slave settlements such as Puerto Tejada. The region has been the setting for historic conflicts such as that of the Paez Indians under the guidance of Quintin Lame; or the struggle waged by peasants, commanded by Cenecio Mina. The Pacific coast is inhabited mostly by Afro-Colombians; the hill range and valley of the Cauca River is inhabited by three ethnic races; while the territory which extends along the Western and Central cordilleras and enters the state of Tolima, is inhabited by Indians and mestizos. The inhabitants of this region are patriarchal yet romantic in spirit (as immortalized by writers such as Jorge Isaacs, Julio Arboleda and César Conto), who propitiated the modernization of agriculture and industry. Lovers of sports and pachanguero music, hard-working, traditional and liberal, they make up one the most contrasting and interesting mosaics in Colombia.

VALLE DEL CAUCA

The state of Valle is today one of the most properous and dynamic regions of Colombia. It can be divided into four areas with different characteristics: 1. The Pacific plains where there are two large bays lined with mangrove swamps: Málaga and Buenaventura. 2. The area which includes the Western Cordillera, with high points such as Los Farallones de Cali; 3. In the central part lies the Cauca River Valley, considered to be the principal area of the state (from which it takes its name), with some of the most fertile lands in the country. It is densely populated with a notable development in agroindustry, principally sugar-cane. 4. The last zone is formed by the western slopes of the Central Cordillera, which makes up the large natural region of Quindío, where the coffee industry is the principal economic activity.

Before the Spanish presence in America, these lands were inhabited by numerous Indian tribes, including the Noamanes, Incuandes, Catíos and Chocoes, in the Pacific region, and Quinchías, Jamundíes, Calotos, Lilís and Quimbayas, in the Andean region.

The first Spanish contingent to arrive in the region was com-manded by Sebastián Belalcázar in 1535; followed by Juan Badillo, Jorge Robledo and Lorenzo de Aldana in 1538, and Pascual de Andagoya and Juan de Ladrilleros in 1539.

In colonial times the territory belonged to the governance of Quito and the province of Popayán. After Independence, in 1821, it became part of the state of Cauca until 1910, when the state of Valle del Cauca was created, with Cali as its capital.

The economy of the state is one of the most solid in the country and revolves around industry, commerce, services, agriculture and cattle ranching, complemented by fishing, mining and lumbering. The main industries are foodstuffs, liquor, textiles, shoes, clothing, chemicals and pharmaceuticals, furniture, leather, rubber, paper, plastic goods, soaps and detergents, and agricultural machinery. Agriculture is well developed and is one of the most prosperous in the country, with sugar-cane plantations, coffee, corn, cotton, sunflower, beans, rice, yucca, grape, plantain, cacao, potato, tobacco, sesame, soya, peanut, aniseed, flowers, fruit, and vegetables. Its lovely

Page 260, Cauca River and a sugar cane plantation.

Page 261. Pacific railroad.

landscape, plentiful rivers, and climatic and topographical contrasts make tourism another source of income for the state. The saying «Valle is Valle and the rest are hillsides» amply reveals the self-esteem of the inhabitants of this region, blest by nature.

CALI

Santiago de Cali, the capital of the state of Valle del Cauca, was founded by Sebastián de Belalcázar in 1536 in the territory of the Calima Indians. Its regional importance is relatively recent since before the beginning of the present century Popayán held sway over the south-west of the country. In spite of being situated in the rich Cauca River Valley in the foothills of the Western Cordillera, the importance of Cali is due to its strategic location as a point of access to the Pacific Ocean. Since commencing the construction of the road to the sea (in which the enthusiastic young man Jorge Isaacs collaborated, and who on the banks of the Dagua River began to write his novel 'María' around the middle of the past century), the importance of Cali has continued to increase.

In 1860, Cali was already the center of crafts manufacture in the region and began to generate a new agricultural economy around the town.

Families left their haciendas for the city with their servants, including slaves who took charge of domestic chores. Traders from all parts of the country and commercial representatives from different countries arrived. Perhaps the most famous of these businessmen was the North American-Russian James Eder, «Don Santiago», who pioneered the state's sugar refining industry. Don Santiago bought the hacienda 'La Manuelita', which belonged to Jorge Isaacs's family, to develop an industrial project of great importance for the region, and for which he brought in modern machinery by mule. Eder also became involved in the growing and trading of tobacco and in exporting coffee.

But none of this would have been achieved without an effective route to the sea or a communications network with the main markets. First the road from Dagua to Buenaventura was widened, then a railroad to the port was constructed, and subsequently a railroad connection to the center of the country was laid; and finally, in this century, a road with excellent specifications linking Cali to Buenaventura, and Cali to the rest of the country was built. From then on, Cali took up the regional leadership. Throughout the state of Valle's history, three other towns in addition to Cali have been links in the chain of development of the region: Palmira, Buga and Cartago. Palmira competed with Cali for leadership in agriculture; Buga has represented the tradition of the large haciendas, and Cartago is the gateway to regions in the north-west.

The area of influence of the region around Cali, considered a cultural and economic complex, represents a broad territory which covers the states of Valle del Cauca, Cauca, Nariño (and beyond to the state of Putumayo), and much of Chocó. This cultural and economic influence is largely due to geographical location and to the communications network which keeps the region in permanent contact with these areas of the country. The region around Cali concentrates the nation's most important sugar refineries and constitutes one of its largest industrial zones, to the point that Cali is Colombia's third city in industrial and commercial importance.

Cali is notable for its cultural activity, with such dynamic institutions as La Tertulia Modern Art Museum, theaters such as Los Cristales, Teatro Municipal and TEC (Teatro Experimental de Cali), and the Universidad del Valle, among others. Film and video-making

is sufficiently significant that people already refer to the city as Caliwood, in recognition of the work of filmmakers such as Carlos Mayolo, Luis Ospina and others in the regional television station Telepacífico and the nation-wide TV channels; the legendary tradition of Cali's cine-club; and the magazine 'Ojo al Cine', initially under the direction of writer Andrés Caicedo, who titled his book in homage to his place of birth: «Cali, Captivating Kaleidoscope».

22 miles north of Cali, on the road to Cerrito, you reach the Hacienda El Paraíso, where the events of the novel 'María' took place, a classic example of South American romance by Jorge Isaacs, several times adapted for the screen. Towards the south of the city, 3 miles along the road to Jamundí, stands the Hacienda Cañasgordas, the setting for another Colombian novel, 'El Alférez Real' by Eustaquio Palacios, which evokes the era of slavery in 18th century Cauca. And 26 miles from Cali stands the Hacienda Piedechinche, home of the Sugar-Cane Museum, where amidst a beautiful landscape the visitor can learn everything about growing and processing sugar cane, the region's main product.

*Page 264, in the center of Cali stands Caicedo Plaza, where buildings of diverse epoques
surround a space shaded by palm trees; on one side stands
San Pedro Metropolitan Cathedral.*

*Cali is a modern metropolis with an excellent infrastructure; its beneficial climate and the
warmth of its inhabitants make it one of the most lively cities in Colombia. On this page,
panoramic view of the international center.*

Above: the Hermitage is one of the symbols which identify Cali; owing to the development of the city»s architecture, it is today surrounded by modern buildings which contrast with its gothic facade. Below: the magnificent complex of San Franciso, an eighteenth century building, whose tower in pure Mudejar style recalls the architecture of the period of Moorish occupation in Spain.

Because of its high urbanistic and industrial development, Cali is considered the most important city in the colombian southwest.

Throughout its entire history, the Banco Popular has faithfully adopted in its vision and its mission, the fundamental principles of nature. It has understood its teachings and has capitalized on them for the benefit of its customers and all Colombia, and like nature, is present throughout the country, a country which is always near a Banco Popular.

The church and convent of La Merced, built in the 17th century, are located in the city»s historical center; the Museum of Archeology and Colonial Art functions here.

Below: La Tertulia Modern Art Mueseum, located on Colombia Avenue, is one of the most important cultural centers in the city; its gallery and museum house a permanent collection of paintings and sculptures by renowned artists.

La Nacional, changed the concept of the book store which until that moment had existed in Colombia. He put the books within the reach of the public, which exhibited in comfortable and functional furniture and bookshelves, allow free access to them. He also introduced in the book store something truly novel: a cafeteria where customers can enjoy a delicious icecream or a comforting café.

With the book stores consolidated in Baranquilla and Cartagena, bookseller Ordóñez moved to Cali to introduce the model which had enjoyed such great success. In Caicedo Plaza, at the heart of Cali, the first Librería Nacional was born in that city, with all the attractions which its unmistakable character

had provided. Other branches followed. Today there are eight book stores which covere all the strategic points of Cali.

Shortly after the opening of the Librería Nacional in Unicentro in Bogotá took place, the most important of them all which sells the most books in the entire country. Subsequently new branches have been opened in Bogotá, in such important spots as the Andino shopping mall, the Hacienda Santa Bárbara shopping mall, the Puente Aereo, and on the carrera 7 in the city center.

The Librería Nacional is today the only chain of bookstores in the country with national coverage and permanent and sustained progress.

Banco Superior. More than what one expects from a bank. The inhabitants of Valle del Cauca know that well since they have 5 offices in Cali, one in Palmira and another in Tuluá, where they can obtain the best financial services: Cuenta Superior, a complete banking portfolio; Diners Club, the leading credit card in Colombia, and excellent financing options for every need.

To the north of Cali stands El Paraíso Hacienda, the setting for «María», the famous novel
by Jorge Isaacs, one of the great expressions of American romanticism. Here there is a
museum where objects which belonged to the writer are preserved, through which the customs
of rural life in 19th century Valle del Cauca can be appreciated.

In Valle del Cauca there are towns whose considerable development during the colonial period
are evidenced in its buildings and in the aristocracy and way of life which its inhabitants
maintain to this day. On this page, the Cathedral of the Señor de los Milagros, in Buga; its
image of the Miraculous Christ is venerated by the Latin American people.

Right: Cartago is a town which preserves architectural jewels of
the colonial and republican eras.

On this page, amid the Eastern Cordillera and close to the town of Darién lies Calima Dam, whose name derives from the culture which occupied this teritory before the arrival of the Spanish. Below, field of sunflowers near Vijes.

Page 275: the Cauca River Valley is one of the most fertile in Colombia: a great variety of crops for food and industrial use, and also fruit trees, are grown; it is also the biggest sugar cane producer in the country.

CAUCA

During colonial times, the province of Cauca was one of the most important regions in the country, due to its proximity to Quito and Lima and its access to the Pacific Ocean, as well as being a region rich in resources for agriculture and mining, with abundant indian labor. Physically the different states are very varied, since in addition to being crossed by the Western and Central cordilleras a part of the Colombian Massif is situated in the area. As a result of its topography, the state of Cauca has the entire range of climatic zones, from tropical lands at sea level to the perpetual snow of the Nevado del Huila, the highest point on the Central Cordillera, bordering the states of Huila and Tolima.

A large number of rivers and streams cross the state of Cauca in all directions. The Cajibío, Caquetá, Cauca, Guapi, Patía, Timba y Timbiquí make the area a cradle of rivers. The Cauca River, which gives its name to the state, descends the Cubilete Hills, at 11.700 ft. above sea level, to an elevation of 3.500 ft. where

it forms a valley 10 to 12 miles wide and about 150 miles long between the Central and Western cordilleras. This is the Cauca Valley, whose lands cover the states of Valle and Cauca.

In pre-Hispanic times Cauca territory was inhabited by members of the Jamundí, Pance, Caloto, Paez, Pijao, Patía, and Guanaca tribes. The first to cover the region on horseback was Sebastián de Belalcázar, one of Francisco Pizarro's officers, en route from Peru in search of El Dorado. Belalcázar founded Popayán in 1536 in the Pubén Valley and subsequently discovered the sources of the Cauca and Magdalena rivers. The Emperor Charles V, king of Spain, conferred on Belalcázar the title of Adelantado and Governor-for-life of Popayán, which covered a territory similar to that of the future State of Cauca in republican times. During Independence and the first years of the republic, Popayán continued to be one of the most important cultural and political centers of the country. In 1910, after the states of Nariño, Valle del Cauca, Chocó,

On this page, the chapel of the Hermitage is a beautiful colonial building which was restored after the earthquake in 1983 and one of the places where the inhabitants of Popayán profess their religious faith.

Page 279, the thermal springs of San Juan, in the Puracé National Nature Park, are one of the most beautiful aspects of the vigorous volcanic activity of the Coconuco Hills.

part of Old Caldas and Caquetá were segregated, poet Gullermo Valencia lamented that the Caucanos were left with only «the pasture of their lands».

The main economic activities of Cauca are mining, agriculture, cattle ranching and lumbering. The most notable minerals are gold, silver, sulphur, kaolin, coal, platinum, copper, marble, gypsum, quartz and other minerals. Agricultural products notably include corn, sugarcane, plantain, wheat, coffee, rice, cacao, beans, tobacco, aniseed and potato. Cattle-ranching supplies meat and milk to the local population.

POPAYÁN

Popayán, the state capital, was founded by Sebastián de Belalcázar in 1537, after an extermination campaign against the Pubenza Indians, farmers and weavers who refused to submit to the Conquerors. Before the first year after its founding was out, and for having

reached a high level of development, Popayán was raised to the rank of district with the name of Asunción de Popayán. On June 26, 1538, the kings of Spain granted the Villa de Popayán its coat of arms and the title of «Very Noble and Loyal Town», in consideration of it being the most important settlement in the entire province of Quito. During the Colony, the town was second in administrative importance after Santafé de Bogotá, and one of the most important centers of influence in Colombian history.

Its privileged geographical position, being on the route between Cartagena to the north, and Quito and Lima to the south, permitted Popayán to play a predominant role during the Colony. As a result, Popayán is one of the most traditional and aristocratic towns in Colombia and is one of its principal architectural jewels. After the earthquake of 1983 which destroyed or damaged most of the buildings, the town

emerged again from the rubble with its valuable architecture carefully restored. The capital of the state of Cauca is famous for its holy week celebrations where the Religious Music Festival takes place, an international event of long-standing tradition.

AROUND AND ABOUT

34 miles from Popayán, in a mountainous area of beautiful landscapes lies Silvia, a typical village of adobe houses and a traditional marketplace, known for its crafts production. Its surroundings are inhabited by the Guambiano indian community, which preserves its traditonal way of life and customs. Another of the attractions of the region is the Puracé National Park, which covers an area of over 300 sq. miles where lakes, waterfalls, volcanoes, nevados and thermal springs abound.

The archeological region of Tierradentro deserves special mention. Situated to the north of Popayán, a mile from San Andrés de Pisimbalá, Tierradentro is a broad and rugged

archeological area, today inhabited for the most part by Paez Indians. Amidst beautiful landscapes, the mountain ridges and slopes contain pre-Hispanic funerary constructions. The funerary tombs or hipogeums of Tierradentro are found at sites such as Loma de Segovia, Alto del Duende, El Tablón, Alto de San Andrés and Loma del Aguacate. The tombs are very varied, from shallow ones to broad tombs more than 20 ft. deep. The hipogeums are decorated inside with geometric motifs in red and black on a white background, and with anthropomorphic figures in relief.

Numerous stone statues have also been found in the region with similar characteristics to those of San Agustín, although their relationship has not been precisely determined. Neither is it known for certain if the sculptures belong to the same cultural group as that which dug the tombs, although there is an opinion that they probably are the work of different cultures.

The Clock Tower (facing page) and the Humilladero bridge (on this page), have become the symbols of Popayán, which has preserved, not only the layout of the streets and the colonial architecture, but also its traditions and the ancestry and elegance of the families which make it one of the most aristocratic towns in the country.

The house where the famous poet and politician Guillermo Valencia lived, now the Valencia
Museum, preserves objects which belonged to him, and is where, according to legend, the
thoughtful shadow of the poet continues to pass down its
corridores on nights of the full moon.

Page 283, the church of San Francisco, with its beautiful stone facade, built in 1775, is one
of the architectural jewels of the town. It was carefully restored after being destroyed by the
earthquake of 1983.

The state of Cauca is one of the regions of Colombia where the inheritors of the Indian cultures which inhabited the Colombian Massif, and the descendents of large Spanish encomenderos and hacendados, continue to live. On this page, interior of a hipogeum in Tierradentro, Guambiano Indians in Silvia, the towers of the church of San Juan and the doctrinaire chapel in San Andrés de Pisimbalá.

Page 285, El Bedón waterfall in Puracé National Natural Park, is one of the natural marvels of the state of Cauca.

Nariño

Situated in the extreme south-west of Colombia, the state of Nariño borders with Ecuador, with which it maintains close economic and cultural ties. There are three well-defined regions in Nariño. The first, to the west, consists of the flat plains of the Pacific coast, with heavy rainfall and a hot climate, whose main economic activity is lumbering. The second, at the center, is the Andean region, consisting of the mountain chain of the Andes which on entering Colombia forms the Nudo de los Pastos, from which two great branches go northwards, separated by the Guáitara and Patía rivers. The left branch is the Western Cordillera which has, in the state of Nariño, some volcanoes such as those of Chiles, Cumbal and Azufral; while the right branch, also known as the Central-Eastern Cordillera, broader than the previous one, has high fertile mesetas where the towns of Ipiales and Túquerres are situated, and some picturesque valleys such as that of Atriz, where San Juan de Pasto stands, the state capital. The third region, on the western slopes of the Amazon basin, has virtually unusable steep slopes, the majority covered by humid rain forest. To the east of this region lies La Cocha Lake, the second most important in the country. Nariño has almost 20 volcanoes, some active, which have caused catastrophes in the past; but they have made the earth extremely fertile and doted it with precious stones.

Hydrographically the state of Nariño is divided into two main basins: the western basin, formed by rivers which flow towards the Pacific Ocean, including the Iscuandé, Mataje, Mira and Patía rivers; and the eastern basin, made up of the tributaries of the Putumayo and Amazon rivers which flow towards the Atlantic Ocean, including the Blanco, Afiliadores, Churuyaco, Guáitara and Guamués rivers. There are also several lakes such as La Cocha, Piusbi and Lake Verde, which is situated at the summit of Azufral Volcano and which derives its peculiar color from the sulphur that flows from a cone near its waters.

In pre-Columbian times the territory of Nariño was occupied by numerous Indian tribes, such as the Pastos and Quillacingas on the highland plain, the Sibundoyes in the Guamués Valley, the Tabiles in the Patía Canyon, and the Iscuandés, Telembíes and Tumas on the Pacific plains. The majority of these territories formed part of the Inca Empire, according to cultural remains and to the different dialects of Quechua origin which some of these communities spoke.

The first Conquistador to explore these areas was Pascual de Andagoya, in 1522, with whose information Francisco Pizarro organized the expedition which led to the conquest of Peru, after having found Gorgona Island and

Sanctuary of Our Lady of Las Lajas.

Tumaco Sound. Pedro de Añasco and Juan de Ampudia were the first Conquerors to explore the mountainous region in 1535, commissioned by Balalcázar, who also traversed it in 1536, reaching as far as Popayán. Belalcázar attached the region of Pasto to the Audience of Quito in 1541. After the country's Independence, in 1819, the region became part of the province of Popayán and in 1821, of the state of Cauca. After several administrative changes, in 1904 the state of Nariño was created, with Pasto as its capital.

The economic activities of the state are basically services, agriculture and cattle ranching, complementaed by crafts manufacture and tourism, and to a lesser extent, mining, fishing and lumbering.

PASTO

The state capital, San Juan de Pasto was founded by Sebastián de Belalcázar in 1537, and founded once again in 1539 by Lorenzo de Aldana. It stands at the foot of Galeras Volcano, at 8.300 ft. above sea-level, with a mean temperature of 57oF. Climbing the volcano is relatively easy and its attraction is due to the fact that it is active, sometimes ejecting enormous clouds of vapor. The region surrounding Pasto is basically agri-cultural, predominantly small farms which confer a singular and beautiful contrast on the landscape due to the diverse shades of color which the crops create. The local people are especially appreciated for their characteristic pleasantness and courtesy.

Several rivers cross the district of Pasto: the Alisales, Jurado, Estero, Guamués, Juanambú, Pasto and Patascoy rivers; and La Cocha Lake, the second most important in the country, from where the Guamués river, tributary of the Putumayo, originates.

During the Spanish Conquest, these lands were inhabited by the Hatunllata or Quillacinga Indians. After its doble founding, the town was transferred in 1540 to its present location by Pedro de Puelles, who gave it the name of San Juan de Pasto that it has today. During its first years, the villa of Pasto grew in population, as much because Conquistadors came here from regions such as Quito, Cali and Popayán, as because the first generation of Americans had been born. In 1559, the Spanish Crown gave it the title of town, with all the accompanying prerogatives.

The district of Pasto depends economically on the city for services, commerce and industry, notably those connected with food and bev-

Page 288, domes of the church of San Felipe in the city of San Juan de Pasto, one of the many churches which bear witness to the deep faith of its inhabitants.

Page 289, typical landscape of the region of Nariño, where volcanic activity has produced very rich soils which are used by small farmers for the intensive farming of crops such as potato, sisal and garden vegetables.

erages, and crafts, which are noted for wood-carvings, characteristic laquered objects, wickerwork furniture, hats, pottery and woven goods. Agricultural products include wheat, barley, potato, aniseed and vegetables; dairying and the production of meat and wool are also important.

Places of interest in Pasto include the church of St. John the Baptist, rebuilt in 1669 after an earthquake, notable for the pulpit of St. John, a true colonial jewel in refined Mudejar style; the church of Christ the King, famous for its stained-glass windows; the Cathedral; the Tamaningo Museum, with traditional examples of the region presented in workshops on view to the public; the Alonso Zambrano Museum, with pre-Hispanic jewels and religious images; the Juan Lorenzo Lucero Museum, dedicated to the history of Pasto; and the Mary Díaz Museum, which exhibits antiques and examples of natural history.

Pasto celebrates its traditional Black and White Carnival between the 4th and 6th of January, with processions of floats and disguises along the city streets. A crafts fair

and the Fiestas de la Virgen de la Mercedes also take place.

IPIALES

The district of Ipiales, the second most populous in the state of Nariño, is the nearest town to the Ecuadoran border, and one of the most important centers of pilgrimage in America. Outside the town stands the Sanctuary of Nuestra Señora de las Lajas, a spectacular edifice of republican architecture built at the beginning of the century over the canyon of the Guáitara River, which houses the image of the venerated Virgen de las Lajas. Thousands of tourists and pilgrims from all over visit the sanctuary each year, clear testimony of the piety of the people of Nariño.

The Rumichaca International Bridge over the Carchi River marks the limit between Colombia and Ecuador. Between Ipiales, a mile from the bridge, and Tulcán, the nearest town in Ecuador to the bridge (2 miles away), a great deal of commerce takes place and the culture on either side of the border is quite similar.

Panoramic view of the city of San Juan de Pasto, capital of the state of Nariño. In the background rises Galeras Volcano, one of the most active in the country. In order to study and monitor its activity and make maps of the dangers, it was declared by the International Association of Vulcanology and Chemistry of the Interior of the Earth, as one of the volcanoes of the decade.

In Pasto and the surrounding countryside there are beautiful spots to contemplate: on this page, (above), landscape of the Heart of Jesus, in the background Nariño Park. Doctrinaire chapel of Tescual, one of the twenty-one Indian villages which surround the city.

Below, facade and dome of the church of San Juan Bautista, a colonial building built in 1539, destroyed by an earthquake and rebuilt in 1669.

Every year the carnival of Blacks and Whites is held in Pasto, one of the most traditional and original fiestas in the country. It begins on January 4 with the arrival of the «Castañeda Family»; on the 5th, all the inhabitants of the city paint themselves black and on the 6th, they whiten themselves with flour and talcum powder. Giant carnival figures with large heads parade down the streets, satirizing everything which was the subject of criticism during the year.

Guamuez Lake, better known as La Cocha Lake, is surrounded by tectonic faults. It is situated 30 minutes from Pasto at a height of 10.000 ft. and around it there are magnificent hotels and restaurants. At the center of the lake, one of the largest in the country, stands La Corota, an island which for its natural riches was declared a Sanctuary of Flora and Fauna.

The state of Nariño has preserved its traditions, both Indian and Spanish, in a pure form. Traveling through this region, you discover places and people whose way of life is surprising for its simplicity and authenticity.

Above, the plaza of El Tambo and a peasant woman with her mule loaded with sisal. Below, detail of the vegetation of the páramo and jetty on Guamuez Lake.

On page 295, a sample of a genuine craft, barníz de Pasto, a very old technique which is used to decorate furniture and wooden objects.

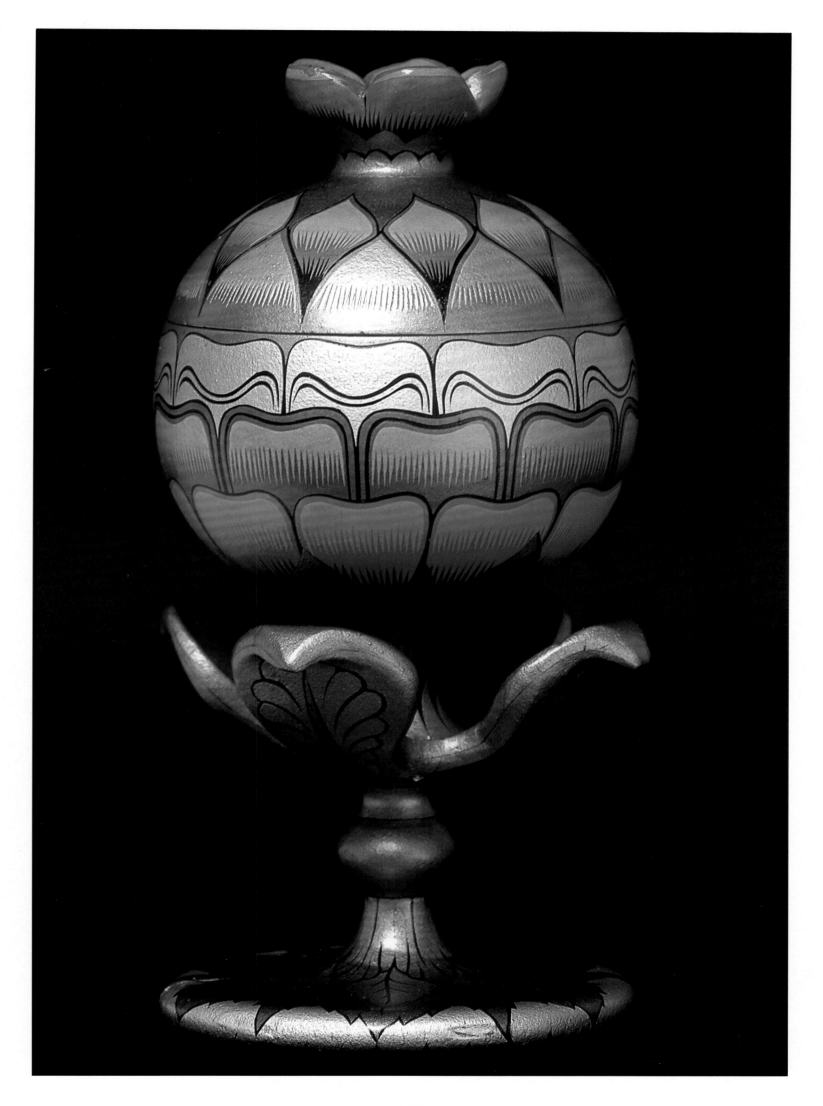

THE UPPER MAGDALENA

*T*he region of the Upper Magdalena, as its name suggests, is situated on the spurs of the Central and Eastern Cordilleras which branch off from the Colombian Massif - in the states of Huila and Tolima - and extend towards the valley which the Magdalena River forms as it flows towards the sea. The Upper Magdalena Valley is the region where the maximum heights of the country's topography are found, with imposing nevados and volcanoes on the Central Cordillera, and fertile valleys where the majority of the region's population is settled. In this part of the country the archeological remains of San Agustín and the reservoirs of Prado and Betania are found. The towns of Ibagué and Neiva are the state capitals of Tolima and Huila, respectively, followed by other nearby towns with which together form an important economic and cultural network which forms a vital part of the nation. Until the beginning of this century,

Valley of the Magdalena River.

these two states made up a single administrative unit known as Tolima Grande.

The inhabitant of this region, which like that of the region of Santander is of Spanish-Caribbean origin, is distinguished from the Spanish-Chibcha mestizo, according to doctor and sociologist Luis López de Mesa, in that he has «a superior stature and aquiline face, with round eyes and nose which curves in a haughty, frank and spirited gesture.» This racial mix of Spaniard and Caribe warrior - Tama, Paez, Andaquí and other indian communities related to these such as the Pijao, Honda, Poinco and Pantágora tribes - partly explains the particular temperament of this ethnic group, which although patriarchal, hospitable, honest and simple, as corresponds to a such a shepherd people as the Spanish, it is at the same time, proud and warrior-like in times of conflict, forthright and loyal at all times, liberal in politics and a lover of equality and justice, as corresponds to their Indian warrior lineage.

The people of Tolima, called *opita*, are zealous guardians of traditional music and national folklore, as evidenced in the state's excellent academies. From this special mix have emerged such eminent and versatile figures as Diego Fallon, musician, mathematician, and poet, well-known for his poem to the Moon; Manuel Murillo Toro, the enterprising and visionary politician; Raúl Mahecha, the revolutionary trade unionist and printer of the 1920s in Colombia; José Eustacio Rivera, the entrepreneur and writer of 'La Vorágine', which denounced injustice in the Amazon and lauded the lushness of the tropics. In contemporary literature, the art of Alvaro Mutis has recreated the wild nature of the Coello of Tolima, the delirious setting of the travels of the famous Macqroll.

HUILA

The state of Huila is located in the south-west of the country, in a territory which covers all the climatic zones: from the tropical lands near the Magdalena River to the páramos and perpetual snow on the peaks in the cordillera. Six different natural zones can be distinguished: 1. The central lowland valley, which is hot, almost completely flat, and bathed by the Magdalena River; 2. The Colombian Massif, considered to be one of the most important areas of the country beause it is where the Eastern Cordillera originates, and near its peaks Colombia's great rivers rise: the Caquetá, Patía, Putumayo, Cauca and Magdalena rivers; 3. The valley of the Suaza River, relatively small and flat but very fertile, surrounded by the

In the state of Huila, which forms part of Tolima Grande, traditional fiestas take place, in which couples dance to the rhythm of the Sanjuanero, deftly executing the complicated steps and figures of this dance which goes back to colonial times (facing page).

In la Chamba a very fine red and black pottery has been developed with the same tecniques inherited from the Indians, which has made the region famous (on this page).

Eastern Cordillera and the hills of La Ceja; 4. The area consisting of the eastern slopes of the Central Cordillera, where the Nevado del Huila rises at over 20.500 ft.; ·5. the mountainous area of Sumapaz, located in the extreme north of the state on the border with Cundinamarca; and 6. the area of the western slopes of the Eastern Cordillera, which has barely been exploited.

Numerous rivers flow off the slopes of the cordilleras, including the Aipe, Bordones, La Plata, Magdalena, Páez, Suaza, and Yaguará rivers. The Magdalena River rises in Lake Magdalena, at 11.800 ft., and descends through a confined, relatively short stretch, to flow into the Betania reservoir, at 1.400 ft., which retains the river before it passes through Neiva, the state capital.

Tribes of Caribe origin such as Paeces, Pijaos and Yalcones occupied the territory of Huila when the Spanish arrived. Before these groups, the region was the setting for more advanced cultures such as that of San Agustín, about whose origins and the causes of its decline little is known. Sebastián de Belalcázar was the first Conqueror to arrive here in 1538. The meeting of the two cultures produced violent conflicts and gave rise to the legend of the cacica Gaitana, who obstinately resisted the Spanish.

During the first years of the Colony, these lands formed part of the province of Popayán until in 1610, when the province of Neiva was created. During the time of Independence, the province of Neiva formed part of the state of Cundinamarca until 1831, when it became independent once again. In 1861 it became the Soveign State of Tolima, later the departamento of Tolima. In 1905 the state of Huila was created, separating its territory from Tolima Grande.

The state of Huila is made up of 37 districts, whose main economic activities revolve around services: banking, transport, tourism and public services provided by the State; agriculture, including coffee, rice, yuca, sorghum, and sugar-cane; industry, especially the food and beverages processing plants, and crafts manufacture; and mining, notably oil and natural gas, and minerals such as coal, gold, lead, silver, copper and sulphur.

Huila has important tourist spots such as the

Neiva, the capital of the state of Huila, is one of the two trading centers of the Upper Magdalena region. On one side of Santander Park stands the Colonial Church, a 7th century building, which preseves a log ceiling, adobe walls and brick floors (this page).

Facing page, a detail of one of the monoliths of the Archeological Park of San Agustín, to the south of the state.

San Agustín Archeological Park, with numerous pre-Columbian statues and Indian monuments; the National Nature Parks including the Cueva de los Guácharos (Cave of the Oilbirds), Los Picachos, Nevado del Huila, Puracé and Sumapaz; numerous natural caves; spectacularly beautiful waterfalls; and landscapes of both mountains and plains, which provide a special reception to the visitor, and which make tourism another important aspect of Huila's economy.

NEIVA

The state capital, Neiva was founded first by Sebastián de Belalcázar in 1539 and then by Diego de Ospina in 1612, on the east bank of the Magdalena River. The town is situated at an altitude of 1.600 ft. with a mean temperature of 79oF. The economy of the district is based on agriculutre, notably rice, sorghum, cacao, corn, beans and plantain; cattle ranching and dairying; and commerce which it maintains with the region and the rest of the country.

The district of Neiva covers the ridges of the Eastern Cordillera and the peaks of the Central Cordillera, a broad swatch of land which is divided by the Magdalena River. The ruggedness of the topography gives Huila the entire range of climatic zones. The tributaries of the Magdalena River are the most important rivers of the district, including the Baché, Cachichí, Cajones, Ceibas, Fortalecillas, Loro and Yaya rivers.

In the north of the district lies the Tatacoa Desert. The Adelantado Gonzalo Jiménez de Quesada named it «The valley of sadness», owing to its arid and eroded aspect, and to the hardships he experienced there. In 1539 Juan de Cabrera, commissioned by Belalcázar to found a settlement on these lands, established a village which he called «Villa de la Limpia Concepción del Valle de Neiva», but when the village was becoming consolidated, Indians from the Otás reserve destroyed it. After other attempts to found a settlement, finally in 1612 Diego de Ospina and Medinilla once again established the village, on the site which it occupies today.

During the Colony the town led a normal life, and during Independence was the setting for some memorable events, such as the execution of numerous patriots in the main square on the 26th of September, 1816, during the height of a wave of «Pacification».

The Bambuco Music Festival and Beauty Contest takes place in Neiva between the 24th of June and the 3rd of July, with processions which parade along the Magdalena River opposite the town; visitors from all over the country respond to the invitation to attend these fiestas in honor of St. Peter and St. Paul.

SAN AGUSTÍN

Several aboriginal cultures which settled in Colombian territory disappeared before the arrival of the Spanish, leaving enigmatic traces of their existence. This is the case of the culture which developed in the region of San Agustín, set on the slopes of the Colombian Massif, a volcanic area where the Magdalena River rises. This complex agricultural society of great lithic sculptors, carvers, potters and builders of burial mounds and temples flourished between the first century BC and 10 AD. The different archeological sites are dispersed in an area of 200 sq. miles within the districts of San Agustín and San José de Isnos, amidst a landscape of hills and deep canyons. The major concentration of statues is found in the Archeological Park of San Agustín, where monumental stone carvings of different syles and sizes can be appreciated, including the well-known Fuente de Lavapatas, a ceremonial site notable for its design and water management. Other sites of statues are Alto de los Idolos, Bosque de las Estatuas, El Tablón, Alto de la Pelota, Alto de la Chaquira and Alto de las Piedras, among others.

This village, situated at 6.000 ft. above sea level, was founded in 1790 by Lucas de Herazo y Mendigaña, after being destroyed on several occasions by the aggressive Andaquí Indians. In 1826 San Agustín was raised to the rank of district. Its lands, although mostly mountainous, also have broad flat or slighting rolling areas, mainly on the flood plains of the rivers which cross it. It has a mean temperature of 66°F.

In the opinion of Colombian anthropologist Gerardo Reichel-Dolmatoff, San Agustín is the center not only of one, but several of the most important cultures in America, whose origins have not been completely clarified. What is known is that with the arrival of the Europeans, this region was inhabited by the Andaquí Indians who had nothing to do with their predecessors. Recognized internationally for its historical and cultural importance, the different settings of San Agustín

were declared by Unesco a Heritage of Mankind in 1985.

TOLIMA

There are three topographically distinct regions in the state of Tolima. The first comprises the mountainous region formed by the Central Cordillera, whose peaks serve as a a natural western limit, where the greatest altitudes of the cordillera are attained such as those of the nevados of Huila, Tolima, Quindío, Santa Isabel and Ruiz. The second region is formed by the valleys of the Magdalena and Saldaña rivers, being the most densely-populated area of the state with flat or slightly rolling land, and to the west several terraces and slopes, on one of which stands the city of Ibagué, the capital. This region is characterized by fertile lands on which large irrigation projects have enabled new territory to be incorporated into the economy of Tolima. The third region, in the south-east, is formed by the western slopes of the Eastern Cordillera, characterized by steep, eroded soils.

Numerous rivers cross Tolima, descending from the peaks of the two cordilleras: Ambeima, Cocora, Azufrado, Combeima, Cunday, Gualí, Prado, Saldaña, and Sumapaz, are some of the names of these rivers, which together with numerous streams contribute to making the territory one of the most suitable for agriculture and fishery in the country.

In pre-Hispanic times the region of Tolima was inhabited by Panche, Natagaima and Pijao Indian communities, descendents of the Caribes, who fiercely opposed the establishment of the Europeans in their region. The Pijao Indians were virtually wipe out, and their courage was respected by the Spanish.

Sebastián de Belalcázar was the first Conquistador to arrive, in the year 1538. He was followed by Hernán Pérez de Quesada, Andrés López de Galarza and Francisco Núñez Pedroza, who founded several villages.

During the past century the provinces of Mariquita and Neiva made up the Federal State of Tolima, until 1886 when the departamento of Tolima was created, known as «Tolima Grande», from which the departamento of Huila was later to secede.

The main economic activities of the region of Tolima are based on agriculture (rice, cotton, sorghum, sesame, coffee, sugar-cane, plantain, corn), cattle raising and dairying; industry and agroindustry have experienced notable progress, especialy with respect to foodstuffs, beverages, tobacco, liquor, soaps, leather goods, textiles,

Page 302, Tolima is a state where large agro-industrial companies have been set up which supply a good part of the demand of Upper Magdalena and the interior of the country.

The town of Honda, on the banks of the Magdalena and Gualí rivers, was one of the main ports during the Colony; through it trade between the interior of the country and Cartagena de Indias was moved. In its historical center beautiful buildings of the 17ty, 18th and 19th centuries are found.

clothing, cement, tools and building materials. Commerce is equally active since Ibagué canalizes the goods produced both in the region and in the rest of the country.

In the Magdalena Valley several oil fields are exploited and in the mountainous areas of the west gold, iron, lead, coal, silver, calcite, quarz, mercury and other minerals are mined. Power generation is an important aspect of Tolima's economy. Prado Dam was built for this purpose, as well as for the attraction which its waters provide for visitors.

During colonial times and until well into the nineteenth century Honda was one of the main river ports on the Magdalena, and a place of territorial linkage, since it channeled commerce from Cartagena and Barranquilla to the rest of the country, principally to Santafé de Bogotá. Honda was founded in 1539 by Gonzalo Jiménez de Quesada, and in 1643 Philip IV of Spain granted the town the title of Villa. The port retains the original layout of the town in good

condition, with narrow streets in which you can admire excellent examples of colonial architecture. When coffee replaced quinine and tobacco as the main export product, Honda became one of the main coffee centers in the country. Today it is known as the «City of Bridges» and events which attract visitors to Honda include the River Festival and the Festival of the Subienda, when you can best enjoy the famous *viudo de pescado*, a typical dish of the region.

During the Colony, the region of Mariquita enjoyed great prosperity as a gold-producing center. The town was founded in 1551 as the nucleus of rich deposits discovered by Hernán Vanegas. Its economic fame paralleled its scientific one, since the scholar Mutis chose the town as the center of his naturalist research, in whose memory a Botanical Garden, the House of Mutis, and a Natural History Museum are maintained.

IBAGUÉ

The state capital, Ibagué stands in the foothills of the Central Cordillera at 4.200 ft. above sea-level, with a mean tempera-

The city of Ibagué, the capital of the state of Tolima, has been called the «music capital of Colombia». In the month of June, the Folklore Festival is held, which seeks to preserve autochthonous values from all over the country.

Page 305, panoramic view of the majestic snow-capped peak of Tolima Volcano.

ture of 75°F. The district stretches from the snow-capped peaks of the Central Cordillera to lands bordering the Magdalena River, covering both mountainous terrain and broad plains. The hydrographic composition of the district includes the Alvarado, Cocora, Coello, Combeima, Chipalo, Opia and Romualdo rivers.

The city was founded by Andrés López de Galarza in 1550 near Pijao Indian settlements, to serve as a point of confluence on the road between the governances of Santa-fé de Bogotá and Popayán. From here pacification campaigns were carried out in the region, especially against the warring Pantágora Indians, in response to a petition made before the Real Audiencia by the inhabitants of Tocaima and Santafé. Once settled, in 1606 Ibagué was granted the category of district. In 1887 it was designated the capital of the state of the North, which formed part of the State of Tolima; and since 1910, when the state of Tolima was created, Ibagué was chosen as its capital.

The imposing Nevado del Tolima rises above the city to the north. The main economic activities of the district of Ibagué revolve around commerce, industry, agriculture, cattle ranching, and mining. The city has a dynamic commerce for being a strategic point on the country's road network and the economic hub of Tolima. The manufacturing industry is well developed with large factories producing foodstuffs, beverages, liquor, metal furniture, cement and building materials; and also coffee processing plants.

Called the «Musical City of Colombia» for its festivals and one of the most renowned conservatories in the country, the National Folklore Festival and Beauty Contest are held in Ibagué between the 20th and 24th of June, on St. John's day, to the sound of bambucos, *torbellinos*, *rajaleñas*, *guabinas*, popular dancing, beauty queens, processions, *matachines* and local food.

To the south of the state of Huila stand the vestiges of the San Agustin culture, one of the
most advanced in working volcanic rock. Previous page,
triangular face on Mesita B of the Archeological Park.

Below, detail of Piedrapintada, an enormous rock with figures engraved on it,
in Aipe, to the north of the state.

Above, the Magdalena River, which rises in the Hydrographic Star of Colombia, crosses the state of Huila; to the south, imprisioned between rocky outcrops, the river snakes down the Central Cordillera towards the valley floor and Betania Dam, a reservoir which uses the waters of the Magdalena and Yaguará rivers, covers 17.000 acres and generates 500.0000 kilowatts of electricity. It has excellent facilities for watersports.

Below, a field of rice in the Magdalena River Valley and La Tatacoa, a desert which covers 130 sq. miles, at 109 °F, and with fascinating landscapes which make it one of the most arid and wildest regions of the country.

In the state of Huila there are pretty villages which preserve their traditional architecture, such as El Hobo, Garzón, Gigante, Pitalito and Suaza.

«The Ceiba of Liberty», one of the attractions of the village of Gigante, was sown by José Hilario López in 1851 to symbolize the freeing of the slaves, decreed by Law of the Republic that same year and leaving Neiva, to the south, there is an immense pavilion of giant trees which provide shade and coolness on the route through the hot valley of the Magdalena River.

ORINOQUIA

*A*ccording to the chronicler Friar Pedro Simón in his Noticias Historiales about Orinoquia, the «land of the rising sun», Bochica, the civilizing god of the Muiska Indians of the highland plain, appeared and taught them to spin, weave blankets, dye cloth and make pottery, and gave them moral, social and political precepts. «...It is said that he came from the east, from the so-called plains of the Llanos which are a continuation the Venezuelan plains, and entered this kingdom at the village of Pasca...» the chronicler relates, who thereby recorded part of the Indian cosmology which the Spanish encountered on arriving in the New World.

Sunset on the plain.

The Llanos does seem to be the land of the rising sun: the impressive beauty of the dawn, the unending grassland plains and the indomitable spirit of its inhabitants are just some of the characteristics evoked by poets such as Eduardo Carranza or musicians and composers such as Arnulfo Briceño and so many others who to the sound of the harp and guitar reaffirm the idiosyncracy of one the most representative regions of Colombia, a folklore and culture that is shared with neighboring Venezuela.

The *llanero* is of mestizo blood, adventurous in spirit and a lover of liberty and of the vast open spaces, and is distinguishable by the three elements which always accompany him: «a good horse, a good saddle, and a good rope to lasso with» as the ballad goes, one of the many songs which to the sound of the joropo, the galerón or the corrido, enliven local celebrations and describe the region.

The vast plain known as the Llanos spreads out from the foothills of the Eastern Cordillera and merges with the savannas of Venezuela and to the south with the Amazon. The region, called Orinoquia because it is drained by all the rivers which flow into the Orinoco River, covers 167.600 sq. miles, equivalent to 38.5% of the country. Its area as a natural region is smaller, since it specifically embraces the flat lands known as the Llanos Orientales with an area of 89.150 sq. miles, representing 20% of the country. Four states make up the Colombian Orinoquia: Meta, Casanare, Arauca and Vichada.

The upper part of Orinoquia is demarcated by the Arauca and Meta rivers, the eastern limit by the Orinoco and Atabapo rivers, the west by the highest part of the Eastern Cordillera, and the south by the Guaviare and Inírida rivers. The vegetation of the savanna predominates, with grass and bushes, scrub and riverside jungle. Large areas are flooded during the wet season and provide appropriate environments for aquatic birds. In the foothills of the Eastern Cordillera there are rain forests with towering trees.

Six different ecosystems are found in Orinoquia. The foothills, a band of sloping land whose height varies between 650 and 3.300 ft. above sea-level, is the most populated, urbanized and exploited part, and possesses some of

Facing page, the Orinoco River basin is partly made up of the innumerable streams and rivers which come off the Eastern Cordillera, such as the Manacacías River, in the state of Meta.

The Meta River is one of the principal means of communication in the Colombian Orinoquia. On this page, Puerto Gaitán.

the richest oil wells in the country. The rivers of a part of Orinoquia prone to flooding, north of the Meta River, burst their banks during the rainy season and cause cyclic flooding. The river system of non-floodable Orinoquia covers the states of Meta and Vichada and is less complex than that of floodable Orinoquia. The Orinoquian Terrace, a strip of land bordering the Orinoco and the mouth of its tributaries, is composed of outcrops of the Guayanese Shield called tepuys, which in Indian tongue means mountain. The hill range of La Macarena, a formation which is independent of the Andes and Guayanese-Brazilian systems, is notable for its ecological riches. And the Transitional Rain Forest links Orinoquia to the Amazon and possesses characteristics of both systems.

Traditionally the economy of Orinoquia has been based on farming, notably cattle rearing with zebu stock, sorghum, and sesame and African palm for the production of natural oils. Fishing in the numerous rivers is another important resource in the region. During the last few years, enor-

mous deposits of oil and natural gas found in the states of Arauca and Casanare have opened the region to big challenges and new economic activities.

When the Spanish arrived, the Orinoquia was populated by different nations of the Arawak linguistic family. Groups of the Chibcha family which inhabited the highlands had come down off the Eastern Cordillera and settled in the foothills, where they began to barter with the Arawaks, a process which was interrupted by the Spanish Conquest. The area was also inhabited by Guahibo nomads who occupied the basins of the Meta, Tomo and Tuparro rivers.

The region of the Llanos also formed part of the legend of El Dorado, and in the sixteenth century Jorge Spira and Nicolás de Federmán organized expeditions to search for the evasive gold. However, penetration of the territory really took force with the establishment of Jesuit missions in Casanare, in spite of resistance by some Indian tribes. In the eighteenth century, Spanish missionaries settled in upper Orinoquia and in 1754 founded the village of Maypures. In 1757 the Jesuits founded San Fernando de Atabapo at the confluence of the Atabapo, Orinoco and Guaviare rivers, to stop the Portuguese from entering the region.

The German scientist Alexander von Humboldt and French botanist Aimé Bonpland are among the most notable travelers and researchers of the Orinoquia, who went up the Orinoco River and marvelled at the rapids, with their foaming torrents, cascades, whirlpools and islands.

The people of the Llanos, bold and intrepid and lovers of the liberty which the vast plains inspire, played a fundamental role in the fight for Colombia's independence from Spain. Although they participated in the comuneros movement, forerunner of the struggle for independence, their great historic act took place during the liberation campaign, when troops commanded by the Spanish general Barreiro confronted the patriot army under the command of Simón Bolívar. After an arduous crossing of the Eastern Cordillera and

the páramo of Pisba, on the 25th of July, 1819, colonel Rendón and his 14 lancers of the Llanos defeated the Spanish army at the battle of the Pantano de Vargas. A few days later, on August 7, the people of the Llanos helped win the final victory of the patriots, with which Colombia's independence was definitively sealed. As a tribute, an imposing sculpture by Rodrigo Arenas Betancourt allusive of this heroic deed was erected at Paipa, in the state of Boyacá.

In modern times the guerrillas of the Llanos became famous when the local people led by such legendary leaders as Guadalupe Salcedo, Eduardo Franco Isaza, the Fonseca brothers, Dumar Aljure and many more, took up arms in the name of the Liberal party, in the violent inter-party strife which bled the country in the 1950s. The first objective of pacification was the Llanos Orientales, and once the Conservative government of Laureano Gómez had been deposed, General Gustavo Rojas Pinilla amnestied the guerrillas of the Llanos. In September, 1953, the guerrillas put down their arms, handing them over to the mili-

tary authorities in different parts of the region. Peace remained elusive, however, and there followed a period characterized by what was called banditry, the social result of the violence and uprooting of so many years of struggle. During recent years, another kind of conflict has scourged a large part of the region, as a result of drug trafficking and subversion.

The state of Meta consists of five distinct geographical regions: the Andean region, the foothills, Orinoquia, the mountain range of La Macarena and part of the Amazon. The drainage area is formed by the basins of the Meta, Guaviare, Guarrojo, Planas and Iteviare rivers, and by sub-basins and lakes.

The area was inhabited by groups of Arawak and Guahibo Indians, who mixed racially to eventually become the llanero prototype. The population of Meta has been subjected to permanent immigration by colonizers who came to occupy lands which until the beginning of the twentieth century were common land, attracted initially by the extraction of quinine and rubber, then wood, and later agriculture. Cattle-ranching is a complement to agriculture in the exploitation of land in the state and produces a large part of the meat consumed in the Andean region.

Villavicencio, the capital of the state of Meta, stands in the foothills of the Eastern Cordillera and is the «gateway to the Llanos». It was founded in 1840 by Estéban Aguirre, becoming a district in 1960. 70 miles distant from Bogotá, Villavicencio channels the majority of the commerce between the Llanos and the rest of the country. The pillars of the economy of the district are commerce, agriculture - especially rice, yucca, corn, sorghum, cotton, cacao and plantain - cattle ranching and oil production, and on a smaller scale, industry, fishing and lumbering. Villavicencio is home to the international tournament of *coleo*, a sport practised in the Llanos of both Venezuela and Colombia which represents the work done when an animal bolts from the herd and the horseman grabs it by the tail and brings it down.

The town of San Martín is an important cattle center and every year the famous cuadrillas are held here, a mix of popular music, folklore and choreography. Puerto López, on the banks of the Meta River, is the main port of the state.

To the south west of the state of Meta rises the National Nature Park of La Macarena, of great scientific value for its tremendous biodiversity, with species from the Andes, Orinoquia and the Amazon.

The state of Casanare ranges from the lowlands of the savanna to the Andean mountains. The exploitation of oil has stimulated economic development in the region, also known for the cultivation of African palm, rice and sorghum. The original inhabitants of Casanare, the Indian tribes of the Achaguas, Tunebos, Guahibos, Támaras, Piapocos, Caquetíos, and Cusianas, fell victim to the Spanish and German conquerors. Religious missions were later established in the region, notably by the Jesuits, Dominicans and Augustinians. The Jesuits converted the Indians and taught them to work in forges amd looms, cultivate, and look after cattle.

Yopal, the state capital, is an important center of commerce in the region, and a starting-out point for the entire Llanos. Paz de Ariporo, also located in Casanare, was founded in 1953 as a result of the armistice when the guerrillas of the Llanos handed over their arms.

Situated in the northern part of Orinoquia, the state of Arauca borders to the north and east with Venezuela. Its most important waterway is the Arauca River, which serves as a border with Venezuela for much of its length and flows into the Orinoco river. This region is one of the richest in bird species in Orinoquia and has a contrasting relief with high Andean peaks and lowland savannas, having a variety of vegetation. When the Spanish arrived, the area was populated by groups of Arawak and Guahibo Indians on the plains and Chibchas in the Eastern Cordillera. During colonial times an important process of mestizaje took place which continues to this day.

In 1983 a promising oil well was discoverd at Caño Limón in the state of Arauca, and shortly afterwards the government announced the existence of vast oil reserves in the region. Colombia joined the group of oil exporting countries, and oil production and the construction of a pipeline to transport the crude greatly stimulated the economic activity of the region.

Arauca, the state capital, is a river port on the border with Venezuela, and an active center of commerce and cattle. During the last few years its economy has grown rapidly thanks to the oil industry. The town of Tame, founded in 1625, has been called the «birthplace of liberty», since it was here that Bolívar decided to cross the Andes to take the Spanish by surprise.

The state of Vichada, whose hydrography is determined by the Orinoco River and its tributaries, has a considerable Indian population. Amazon-type vegetation is found in the southern part while the rest of the region corresponds to Orinoquia. Puerto Carreño, founded in 1922, is the capital of the state, its economy being based on commerce, fishing and some cattle ranching.

In the district of Puerto Carreño lies Tuparro National Nature Park, covering an area of 1.890 sq. miles, where several species of primates, birds, reptiles and fish are found.

Colombia's Llanos Orientales are immense savannas which stretch from the foothills of the
Eastern Cordillera to the border with Venezuela. On the previous page,
sunrise over the plain, seen from the Sierra Nevada del Cocuy.

The morichales and woodlands —are small patches of vegetation on the savanna, suitable for
the development of a rich biodiversity. They owe their name to the moriche palm, under whose
shade other species grow— and Sunset over the Ariari River, in the south of the state of Meta.
In spite of development and progress in the means of communication, it is still possible to
travel the way early settlers and explorers of past centuries penetrated this isolated region.

The broad savannas are apt for cattle ranching, the main source of work for the inhabitant of the Llanos, whose free and indomitable character is reflected in his work-style and in his folklore, customs and traditions. He is the descendent of the legendary lancers who sealed Colombia's independence from Spain.

Villavicencio, the principal city of the Colombian Orinoquia, called the «gateway to the Llanos», is connected to Santafé de Bogotá by an excellent highway which is considered to be one of the most accomplished works of engineering in the country; much of the agricultural products and cattle which supply the capital are moved along it.

On this page, one of the most beautiful sights provided by nature in the Llanos are its marvelous sunsets and foothills in the state of Casanare, where the cordillera gently slopes down and merges with the plains. It is the region where the most recent oilfields in the country have been found.

On the following page, the Arauca River, part of whose course marks the border with Venezuela.

waterlily in the world. Pink dolphins can be admired in some of its rivers, and in the jungle it is possible to come across the anaconda, a colossal serpent which can measure up to 30 ft. in length. It is paradise to those who love unspoiled nature, since it has the greatest number of species of flora and fauna known to Man. But it is also a «green hell» which reacts aggressively towards intruders who fail to show it respect, the jungle which Arturo Covo, the protagonist of the novel La Vorágine, ventured into.

It is a sparsely-populated region inhabited by Indian tribes such as the Ticunas, Huitotos, Mayuranas and Ocainas, which continue to preserve their myths, rituals and ancestral traditions. But it has also been a region which has received all kinds of people from the four corners of the nation who have migrated here in search of riches and opportunities or are fleeing from difficult situations of poverty and violence. The intricate relationship between history, geography, colonization and State action or inaction which give rise to such conflicts have been clearly postulated by Alfredo Molano in his different literary works, essential

to understanding the problems of this vast and enigmatic region.

Of the Amazon's total area, which with its 2.6 million sq. miles is the richest rain forest on Earth, 155.600 sq. miles belong to Colombia, equivalent to 35.4% of the nation. Six large states make up the Colombian Amazon region: Amazonas, Caquetá, Putumayo, Guainía, Guaviare and Vaupés.

The Amazon region, which extends towards the southern limit of the Llanos Orientales, is for the most part a vast plain covered by dense jungle, irrigated by a large number of rivers. The main one is the Amazon River, the second in the world for its length and the first one for the volume of its flow of 120.000 cubic meters per second. Of its total length of 3.897 miles, 71 miles pass by the extreme south of Colombia in what is known as the Amazonic Trapeze. In the wet season the river is a mile wide opposite the Colombian port of Leticia.

It is not easy to determine the Amazon's distant past, since climatic conditions and jungle soils make the preservation of historical remains difficult, although interesting rock carvings have been found, notably in the south

Facing page, sunset on the Amazon River, the river with the largest volume of water in the world. The river bank belonging to Colombia is only a little more than sixty miles long and at its southern end stands Leticia, the capital of the state of Amazonas and the main town in the Colombian Amazon.

This region has been called the lungs of the planet owing to the lushness of its virgin jungle, whose canopy is so dense that in many parts it obstructs the sun's rays (below).

of the state of Caquetá. It is believed, however, that the presence of Man goes back for thousands of years.

Primitive inhabitants, the majority of the Arawak Indian group, probably settled along the main rivers over 12.000 years ago and must have been quite numerous, although no estimate of the population at the time of the arrival of the Spanish has been made. Today, the Indian population of the Colombian Amazon is no more than 70.000, divided into many different groups and linguistic families. In spite of the presence of Man for thousands of years in this region, the Indian inhabitants knew how to adapt to the environment and wisely use the renewable resources of the jungle, without affecting the ecosystem which produces them.

European penetration began in the sixteenth century. The first conqueror to enter the Amazon was Francisco de Orellana, around 1524. He commenced his exploration down the Amazon River, to which he gave its name for the native warriors which were said to inhabit the re-

gion and which reminded him of the legendary Amazonas, female warriors of Ancient Greece.

In 1541, Hernán Pérez de Quesada organized one of the most ambitious expeditions undertaken in America in the search for the mythical El Dorado. The expedition, which crossed the cordillera before entering the jungle, was composed of 5.000 Indian bearers, 270 Spanish and 200 horses, the majority of whom died.

During the Colony, the colonization of the jungle was undertaken by religious communities, notably Jesuits, Capuchins and Franciscans, who during the 17th and 18th centuries founded missions which suffered numerous attacks from Indians. At this time, incursions by Portuguese traders who hunted for Indians to enslave them were common. Colonial governors and early republicans showed scant interest in the jungle and as a result it remained almost intact until the end of the 19th century. During the 1870s collectors of quinine, Colombia's first important export

The rivers of the Amazon create seasonal lakes which owing to the isolated nature of the water's flow they become ideal spots for fishing (below).

In this ideal natural environment, an immense variety of animal and vegetable species have developed which constitute the princial biological reserve in the world.

Facing page, howler monkey.

product, began to penetrate the basins of the Caquetá and Putumayo rivers.

In 1875, General Rafael Reyes, who later became president of Colombia, founded together with his brothers, the first commercial enterprise dedicated to the extraction of quinine and rubber, destined for European markets. It was a difficult undertaking, with workers brought from the interior of the country, many of whom succumbed to yellow fever. Finally, the bonanza ended when the Europeans began to plant the tree in Asia. However another bonanza was to begin, that of rubber, the source of much suffering in the region.

At the beginning of the 20th century, the developed nations began to use rubber for manufacturing tyres and its price rose steeply. Thousands of settlers came to the jungle in search of their fortune, giving rise to crude stories such as those which José Eustasio Rivera related in La Vorágine (1924). A Peruvian trader, Julio César Arana, set up the first large-scale rubber extractions in the Putumayo region, subjecting Huitoto Indians to forced labor.

Over a period of twenty years, the Casa Arana built an empire and wiped out 80 per cent of the Indian population in the Putumayo region.

In 1922 the Lozano-Salomón treaty which established the Amazon border between Colombia and Peru was signed, and Leticia became Colombia's port on the Amazon. The treaty created serious problems for the Casa Arana, whose facilities were well inside Colombian territory. The rubber barons unsuccessfully tried to stop the treaty from being approved, and then obliged their Huitoto slavaes to migrate to Peru.

In 1930 General Sánchez Cerro deposed the president of Peru and not long afterwards a group of Peruvians, supported by the government, expelled the Colombian authorities from Leticia. The conflict between Colombia and Peru led the government to exercise its sovereignty over the Colombian Amazon, and assigned a budget for a military presence and the building of infrastructure in the region. In 1931, as a result of a protocol, Leticia and the Amazon Trapeze were definitively ratified as part of Colombia.

Road building facilitated the process of colonization, notably cattle-rearing, which began in the foothills of the state of Caquetá. In the 1950s, inter-party violence which spread throughout the country displaced large numbers of the population, many of whom moved into the states of Caquetá and Putumayo.

Hunting for animal skins and cutting down the best tree species for fine woods accelerated immigration and began the systematic destruction of the jungle. In 1962 the agrarian reform institute, INCORA, with a view to channeling «spontaneous colonization» stimulated the building of roads, health facilities and schools, and supported a model of colonization based on farms of 120 acres for agricultural production and cattle-ranching. However, this tended towards the creation of large farms, where big landowners and cattle ranchers began to buy up the land, now cleared of jungle, from the original settlers.

In recent years, the cultivation of marihuana and later the sowing and processing of coca, became the new bonanzas of the region, endangering the fragile jungle soils. Although the Government has instituted a forceful erradication campaign, jungle conditions make the detection of the crops difficult and encourage the activities of another destabilizing element: guerrillas. These circumstances complicate the social situation of the region, whose inhabitants end up falling victim to forces in conflict and suffer from the problems which easy money generates in the long term and from the inflation which results from excessive enrichment, in detriment to traditional crops.

Today, the Colombian Amazon, with respect to both its people and its natural resources, generates greater interest on the part of governments, at last aware of the importance of preserving not only the jungle soils, but the entire ecosystem, that is to say, the interrelation between climate soils, water, flora and fauna. There is a much greater environmental awareness, with the concepts of sustainable economic development and ecology prevailing. Only by taking such a path will it be possible to preserve the vast area of the Amazon, whose benefits cover the globe.

The state of Amazonas, situated in the extreme south west of Colombia and sharing borders with Brazil and Peru, is covered by dense jungle and drained by numerous rivers and streams. In pre-Columbian times it was inhabited by diverse Indian tribes, notably Arawaks, Tucanos, and Karibs, of which various groups of descendents, such as the Tikunas, the Curripacos, the Cubeos and the Carijonas survive today.

Amazonas has the characteristic topography of the plains of the Amazon without significant variations in altitude. The most important rivers which flow through the region include the Amazon (which in Colombia passes through the Amazon Trapeze), and the Putumayo, Caquetá and Apaporis rivers. Although It has a very varied vegetation, its soils contain few nutrients and require special care since crops rapidly exhaust them.

The state's economy revolves around fishing, lumbering, rubber extraction, commerce and ecological and adventure tourism. The Amacayacu National Nature Park is found here, covering an area of 1.130 sq. miles, rich in animal and vegetable species.

Leticia, the capital of the state and a port on the Amazon, was founded in 1867 by a Peruvian captain Benigno Bustamante, governor of the District of Loreto. A treaty which resolved border disputes between Colombia and Peru ratified Colombia's claim on Leticia. Recently groups of scientists and environmentalists in Leticia have focused their interest on the potential for research and appropriate technologies for the region, with a view to build a model of development for the Colombian Amazon.

At the close of the past century, settlers from the interior of the country reached the state of Caquetá in search of quinine bark, which at the time was much in demand in foreign markets. Later when the market for quinine collapsed, the selvatic southern part of Caquetá participated in the rubber boom. Around 1945 the first large farms appeared in the fertile lands of the Andean foothills. At the same time, groups of settlers penetrated the dense jungle felling trees to sell the wood. Colonization produced rapid erosion in many regions. Today, the sowing of grass adaptable to the fragile earth and been recovering unproductive land.

The Amazon is where one of largest variety of species on Earth is found, species which in addition to their beauty, are of great use to Man.

Facing page, heliconia, a flower of strange shape and singular color. On this page, the tangled vegetation of the Amacayacu National Nature Park, where the foliage of a multitud of vegetable species intertwine.

In 1902 Florencia, the state capital, was founded, situated in a fertile area drained by the Orteguaza, San Pedro and Bodeguero rivers. Very near Florencia, at a place called El Encanto, stands an enormous bas-relief carved in the rock with figures of snakes, lizards and monkeys, one of numerous examples of rock carvings and paintings which have been discovered in different parts of the Amazon.

The state of Putumayo runs from the western foothills of the Eastern Cordillera to the Amazon plain to the east, and is delimited by two large rivers: to the north the Caquetá River and to the south the Putumayo River. The Spanish penetrated the territory in the sixteenth century and in 1551 Pedro de Agreda founded Mocoa, today the state capital. The initial settlements had to face resistance by Inga and Huitoto Indian tribes, whose descendents continue to constitute the majority of the indigenous population.

Like other parts of the Colombian Amazon, the Putumayo re-

gion was the target of expeditions in search of quinine bark, organizaed by General Rafael Reyes amidst all kinds of adversity. The native population fell victim to the rubber fever when the Casa Arana entered these lands to hunt and enslave human labor for the extraction of latex.

Once the border conflict between Colombia and Peru had been resolved, which mainly interested the state of Putumayo, the 1940s and 50s were years of colonization. In the 1960s the production of oil in the area of Orito began, and the builiding of a pipeline drew workers from all over the country. The most developed town of the state is Puerto Asís, founded in 1912 by the Capuchins. It became a military base during the conflict with Peru and then displaced Mocoa in economic growth thanks to its proximity to the oil fields of Orito.

The state of Guaviare is located in the northern part of the Colombian Amazon and is drained by an intricate network of rivers, among them the Guaviare River, formed by the confluence of

This jungle region is one of the most humid in the world, owing to the heavy rainfall and high tempertures. On this page, dawn in the jungle.

On the following page, the foliage of the trees on its banks reflect in the stillness of the waters of Tarapoto, one of the seasonal lakes which are formed by river courses in the rainly season.

the Guayabero and Ariari rivers and which give it its name. This river forms the border between the states of Meta and Vichada and is the divide between Orinoquia and the Amazon. The territory is characterized by flat plains or slightly rolling land with some important hill ranges, such as those of Chiribiquete, San José and Tunahí. Its rivers are divided into two main basins: to the north the so-called «white rivers» rise in the cordillera and end up flowing into the Orinoco River.

To the south, the tributaries of the Amazon, called «black rivers», originate in the jungle. The town of San José del Guaviare is the state capital of a region of colonization which includes the Nukak National Nature Reserve, the home of Makú Indian nomads, and part of the Chiribiquete National Nature Park.

The state of Vaupés, situated in the south east of Colombia on the border with Brazil, is almost exclusively inhabited by Indians of the Cubeo, Desana, Guanano and Tukano tribes. Its larg-

est rivers and prinicipal means of transport are the Apaporis, Cananarí, Macaya, Papunahua, Papurí, Pirá-Piraná, Querarí, Taraira, Tuy and Vaupés rivers. The most important settlements are Mitú, the capital, located on the right bank of the Vaupés River and surrounded by dense jungle, and Carurú and Taraira, two small villages situated on the banks of the Apaporis River.

The state of Guainía consists of dense jungle, drained by numerous rivers with impressive rapids. Puerto Inírida, the capital, was founded by settlers in 1963 with the name of Obando, on the banks of the Inírida River which in 1965 gave it its name.

One of the largest nature reserves in the country is found in the region of Puerto Inírida near the Brazilian border: the Puinawai National Nature Reserve, which covers an area of 4.200 sq. miles and is situated in the hill range of Caranacoa and the surrounding lowland between the Inírida River and the border with Brazil.

The inhabitants of the Amazon depend largely on the rivers, in which fish abound; they are also the only means of communication among the few settlements dispersed along their courses. Facing page, fishermen on the Amazon River. On this page, panoramic view of the great river which at Leticia is over a mile wide.

Amacayacu National Nature Park, near Leticia, is a synthesis of the lushness of the Amazon. On entering the jungle along streams and rivers, you can get to know the immense biodiversity of the most mysterious natural region on Earth. Among the dense vegetation are palm trees such as the guasay and chonta, red and white oaks, and innumerable lesser species which enrich the vegetation cover.

The broad Amazon jungle is shared by Colombia, Peru, Brazil and Ecuador, inhabited by
Indian tribes which continue to maintain their cultures, way of life and ancestral customs
intact and are the habitat of exotic plant and animal species unique in the entire world, some
of them in danger of extinction, which is why we should be committed to protecting the
jungle, considered to be the planet's principal "lung".

Without doubt, the Amazon is one of the places with the greatest biodiversity in the world, and constitutes the principal genetic reserve for the future of Mankind. On this page, one of the 3.000 species of butterflies found in Colombia and an alligator, which inhabits the lakes and rivers of the region. On the facing page, the marvellous Victoria Regia.

This is Colombia, Pablo, with its foam and its stone
sweetly curved on the shoulder of America.

Jorge Rojas